BARBARA JORDAN
A Self-Portrait

Books by Shelby Hearon

BARBARA JORDAN
A Self-Portrait

Barbara Jordan and Shelby Hearon

DOUBLEDAY & COMPANY, INC., GARDEN CITY, NEW YORK
1979

ISBN: 0-385-13599-8
Library of Congress Catalog Card Number 78-2049
Copyright © 1978, 1979 by Barbara Jordan and Shelby Hearon
All Rights Reserved
Printed in the United States of America
First Edition

For our friends

NANCY AND JAN
REED AND ANNE

PREFACE

In March of 1977 mutual friends introduced me to Barbara Jordan in the hope of our working together on a book. We met in the small brown-and-black study of a house outside Austin, in the unpopulated, tree-lined countryside we both call home.

Left alone, in bluejeans over drinks, we talked about place in the family, about mothers as positive and negative role models, about fathers as judges. "I am the oldest of four daughters," I told her.

"I am the youngest of three," she said.

After a time she got to the point. "We are supposed to talk about a book."

"So I understand," I answered.

But we both hesitated. She, as a politician, operated from a basic distrust of journalists; and I, as a novelist, from a conviction that real life is always distorted by bias, that only fiction offers the glimpse of truth.

"I have nothing to say," she stated.

"I have nothing to ask," I responded.

We sat awhile in silence. She was younger, thinner, shyer, incredibly more vulnerable than I had imagined her.

"Well, if you did a book," she asked at last, "how would you see it?"

"Well, if I did a book," I told her slowly, "I see it as how you got from There to Here. Everyone gets from there to here. So everyone can relate to that."

"Where do you think here is?" Suddenly it was the Jordan voice, conveying a lifetime of chips on the shoulder, the expectation of misunderstanding.

I met her dark gaze. "I think here is on the road to Barbara Jordan."

I said *on the road* because for Barbara wheels are the symbol of freedom. The vehicle, as metaphor and fact, is her means of exit and entrance.

I said *here* because Barbara exists and reacts only and always where she is at the moment. She lives as she talks: in the present tense. Her thought process, as her speech pattern, reflects the flattened, linear external form, and the inner sifting and selecting, of Gertrude Stein's prose.

"Do you think I'll ever get there?" she asked.

"No, but I think you'll die trying."

"I want you to do the book."

We present here a continuation of our initial dialogue. Her voice, as she told the story, remains hers; mine, as I have reconstructed the world's perceptions and conceptions of her, remains mine. We feel this view of a singular life, representative of each of us in its complexities and its longings, rings true both in its facts and in its underlying meaning.

                                                      Shelby Hearon

Austin, Texas
1978

"People always want you to be born where you are. They want you to have leaped from the womb a public figure. It just doesn't go that way. I am the composite of my experience and all the people who had something to do with it. And I'm going to try to lay that out."

Barbara Charline Jordan

ONE

BLACK WORLD

"I felt at that time when I was saying, 'I'm not going to be like the rest,' my point of reference was other black people. It seemed an impossibility to make any transition to that larger world out there."

1. GRANDPA PATTEN

I had three bicycles, given to me by my Grandfather Patten. He, my mother's father, was always very dear to me. My mother tells me that she could leave me with him as a baby and I wouldn't whimper, that there was just no problem with that. So that attachment was formed at the beginning.

He was different from the other men in my family because he didn't go to church. On Sunday I was accustomed to seeing my father and my other grandfather in black suits and white shirts and ties, singing in the choir or being the chairman of the deacon board. This grandfather was different in that he was not part of that churchgoing.

I saw him every Sunday, as it was our pattern as a family to get up, go to Sunday school, go to church, and then go to Grandfather Patten's house for Sunday dinner. My Grandmother Patten would prepare a grand meal, and that was a part of the ritual. Then, after dinner, my mother and father would take a nap, and in the afternoon my sisters would have to return to the Baptist Young People's Union

(BYPU). Bennie and Rose Mary, my sisters, wanted to go back to learn their Bible verses and the books of the Bible, but I didn't. So Grandpa would say: "You don't have to do that." And I didn't. So that was the pattern throughout my entire early years.

I stayed on Sunday afternoons to be with him, and we got on famously. Other people said my grandfather was eccentric. I don't think he was: I think other people were. He was just a very independent person. He never wanted a boss, as he always wanted to be his own boss. So much so that he went through several business ventures. I am told he was a preacher at one time, but that there was some event in his life, which I did not know about, that turned him sour on the church. I remember my mother saying at one point that he had had a café. I remember her saying: "Do you recall when he had the café on West Dallas in Fourth Ward?" I told her: "No, I never knew he had a café on West Dallas in Fourth Ward." She said: "I guess you wouldn't recall that." Well, Daddy tried to have this café and be doing good business, so he let them get things on credit; but the folks just ripped him off, I suppose, and he never got paid. So he got out of the café business. Then at a later point he had a confectionery store with cookies and candy and the like.

When I knew him best, those years of my going there every Sunday, he was in the junk business. He had a very large wagon and two mules, which he kept in the heart of the old Fourth Ward, which is now downtown Houston. And the city health authorities were always out there telling him these mules and the rags and the paper and the scrap iron and the manure were an eyesore. The inspectors would come and say, "Clean this up," and he was never cowed by those people at all. White people coming to tell this man you can't keep mules and manure in downtown Houston, and he would just say: "I'll clean it up." He'd get out and he'd kind of shore it up and make it look presentable. He would make a fence out of big pieces of tin or pieces of cardboard that you couldn't see through, to contain things, and he'd write little sayings in red crayon on the cardboard. I remember one big red sign that said THE LORD IS MY SHEPHERD, and another that said THE DAY OF WRATH IS COME, and both were signed "St. John," which was what he called himself, John Patten. So I liked that.

My grandfather would go out in his wagon with the mules into various areas of the city picking up rags and paper and scraps. He would go into River Oaks, and people would leave stuff out for him and he would put it in the wagon and bring it back to the house in Fourth Ward and sort it all out.

And part of my Sunday afternoon experience was to go out into his yard and help him sort out the rags and get them bundled up and get the papers stacked and tied and the metal piled. And we put the manure in baskets and we sold it for fertilizer to those same folks in River Oaks who gave us stuff.

And there was a merchant, a Jewish merchant, that we called Old Man Moses, who came to buy some of the wares from my grandfather, and I would help weigh the rags and things, which we sold by the pound.

And that's interesting, as I haven't seen a scale like that in recent years. It was a vertical piece of metal with a hook on the end, and you could put the bundle on the hook and it would pull down and show you the weight. And that's what we had attached to the back porch. And Old Man

Moses would come and he would sit and I would be in charge of weighing and we'd bundle it up, and he would always pay whatever it was worth.

My grandfather and I, we had it all arranged out there with the businesses lined up and sectioned off along the whole side of the house. And we never were without buyers for all that stuff. I didn't know what happened to Old Man Moses once he left there with the goods. He took it away on a truck, not a wagon like we had.

My grandfather always gave me a part of the money. He always saw that I had some of it. He gave me a money belt which had a little zipper area. You wore it under your clothes and around your waist. So I always had money. I always had more money than Bennie and Rose Mary because, you see, I was in business. Now, Bennie and Rose Mary did not want to do that sort of thing. They felt it was nasty out there in the junk and they wouldn't go out there. They were just little Sunday-school-going kids and BYPUers, and they weren't going to put on old clothes and get down into the horse manure sorting old rags and paper and getting dirty.

And Grandpa would give me money to keep for him. I was his bank. And I tell you, it would be a great wad. Because we had a successful business. We had that.

He really catered to me in every way. There is nothing that he thought I might want that he wouldn't get for me. He gave me a pair of diamond earrings on one occasion. I was just a little kid, and he gave me this pair of diamond earrings which were made for pierced ears. And I didn't have my ears pierced. I told him I really didn't want to have my ears pierced. So he said: "Well, we'll get them made over and do some that screw on your ears." Which he did. He had them made so they'd screw on my ears.

Needless to say, I didn't have much appreciation of a pair of diamond earrings at that time.

Then I decided that I wanted a bicycle. So I asked him if he would get me a bicycle. Well, in his travels to pick up old stuff, someone left out an old, what he called a skinny-tire, bike. He brought that to me and I was glad to have it. But I soon wanted a better bicycle. I said: "Look, I want a brand-new bicycle." So he went to Western Auto and got me a new blue-and-white Schwinn bike. Then I had two bicycles. Later, in his travels, he picked up another one, which he gave to me. So at one point I had three bicycles.

In those days, as a child, I had an extreme dedication to playing. Just the whole game bit. There were a couple of kids who lived on the block and we played all the childhood games. There were pine needles, and we'd gather them together and make a little house. And we'd make dolls out of soda-water bottles. We'd get a bottle and put a piece of rope in the end and that was your doll. We'd play that. Jacks, a great deal of jacks. I liked that, playing hard. I liked having the time to play and I didn't have to wear shoes, and I knew you had to wear shoes when you started to school. I didn't look forward to getting big enough to start school because I knew playtime would be cut short and I wouldn't be able to play as hard as I had been doing. And I did play hard.

But Grandpa didn't want me to be like the other kids. That came through loud and clear. He would say this very directly. There were kids who lived just behind my grandfather's house in Fourth Ward that he did not want me to associate with because he said: "You don't have to be like those others." In relation to other kids he would say: "You just trot your own horse and don't get into the same rut as everyone else."

He did not want me to play with them, but sometimes I would sneak around—I mean literally sneak out—when they were having a birthday party and they had ice cream and cake.

He was speaking for himself as well, because he felt himself quite different, just a little cut above the ordinary man, black or white. That was continually driven into me in those years: Look, this man can make it, my grandfather. He can put together whatever combination of things necessary and just kind of make it. And that had an impact on me.

To this day I carry three pictures of him in my wallet— one in his hat that he wore, one in a barber chair, and one on his wagon. Now, I know he carried several pictures of me, because I found one, and on the back he had scratched out Barbara Charline and written in Barbie Edine, as Charline was for my other grandfather, Charles Jordan, and he wanted me named for him, John Ed Patten.

His house was old. He rented it. He didn't own his house like my other grandfather. It did not have indoor plumbing. There was an outhouse back from it. There wasn't any electricity and I can recall my grandmother ironing with smoothing irons, which you set on the wood stove to get hot. We got water from a faucet off the back porch. We would carry a bucket of water, city water, from there to the kitchen table just inside the door, where there was a tin dipper. In Fourth Ward there were no trees or grass at all, as I recall, because his yard was bare; we swept it clean.

But he always spoke of his family with pride and respect. He always did. He was very proud of his family and he would talk about his father, who was a lawyer in Washington, and I didn't know about that, what that meant, but it just sounded fine.

It was part of the ritual on those Sunday evenings that, when the others had left, we would talk. In those early years it was certainly the case that he was the only one who talked to me—because mostly what adults do to children is to give them catechism in some form or another. But in terms of instructions about how to live, that is missing.

Before we talked, we had to eat. My grandfather would walk two blocks down Matthew Street from West Webster to Matt Garner's barbeque. He would go down there, and of course blacks were not allowed in that kind of barbeque place, but my grandfather would go to the back door of Matt Garner's and get a paper bag loaded with *reg'lars*. If you had a barbeque establishment you had ribs, and when you were cutting them off there was always an end that was left over, that was not fit for serving to a customer, but it was good barbeque. So you had ends of beef and you had ends of ribs and ends of sausage, and Matt Garner would just throw those ends away unless my grandfather came down and got this bag of reg'lars. He'd leave me at his house and he would go get them and he'd come back with this brown paper bag full of meat. And he'd lay it there, and that's what we would eat for our late-night snack. The meat all by itself from a brown paper bag. That was the highlight. I remember it as a super time.

Then we would talk. He would have his Bible and inserts that he had stuck in the Bible, sayings that he would always write in red crayon. And he'd read from those—from the Gospel According to St. John, he'd call them, after himself. He had a saying which I remember as clearly as the day he first read it, and I don't know who wrote it, but he taught it to me and he would make me recite it back to him with some regularity.

> "Just remember the world is not a playground, but a school-room. Life is not a holiday but an education. One eternal lesson for us all: to teach us how better we should love."

That was a very nice sentiment.

So then he would read about the life of Christ. And I could understand Jesus and God better from my grandfather talking than from the church, and that was because he communicated in a language I could understand. He taught me that if I followed his standards, and did what he said, and just followed the plan of action that he set out for me, I would be moving in the path of following Christ. And His path was an overwhelming degree of self-sufficiency—that's a present-day term, but that's the way I perceived it at that point. Grandpa was saying that the message of Jesus is: Don't get sidetracked and be like everybody else. Do what you're going to do on the basis of your own ingenuity. He was also saying that you couldn't trust the world out there. You couldn't trust them, so you had to figure things out for yourself. But you had to love humanity, even if you couldn't trust it. That's what he said the message of Jesus is.

God he presented as the power that controls us all. *Power* was the word that stuck in my mind when I thought about Grandpa Patten speaking about God. He definitely did not present God as a father image. He was always power. That was the operative word.

So we sat and had those lessons on Sunday night.

And I was always very proud of my grandfather. I remember a minister friend of my father's quoting onetime from a passage of scripture about a man who left the church and went down from Jerusalem. He kept talking about how when you leave the church "you go down." Down from Jerusalem.

And I remember thinking: "You idiot. My grandfather's going to be there opening the gates for you."

John Ed Patten grew up with loss and violence. The younger brother of two sons, born in a piney woods settlement east of Houston, called Evergreen, he came to consciousness on the tale of a grandfather killed by a white man. While he was still young, his beloved father abandoned his small sons to go East to become educated and read for the law, leaving John Ed and his brother, Steve, with their mother, and, in the next few years, a new stepfather and six half-brothers and sisters, including a set of twins. Approaching manhood, still aching for his father, he suffered the death of his brother, Steve, in a freak accident at a blacksmith shop. Steve had got into a fight with a man who remarked on his fine horse and wanted to take it, and, in the scuffle, a bullet flung against the grindstone ricocheted into his heart. The family who rushed the bleeding man to a hospital in Galveston found themselves with a corpse on their hands—and sold his body to the medical students.

Grown, on his own, John Ed began again to build a family reflecting the distinction of the Patten name which had produced his father, now a lawyer, and his cousin, the first black woman doctor in Houston. He married Martha Ellen Fletcher; and they had daughters, Arlyne and Johnnie, and a baby son, Ed.

The Fourth Ward, where they lived in the early years of the twentieth century, was a black pocket bordering the heart of the city. In their neighborhood frame houses with asbestos roofs had yards for collards, turnip greens, marigolds, and zinnias; across the ward the funeral home, with its big black limousine and portly director, faced run-down row houses with privies. At the center of the ward were beer halls, pawnshops, barbeque stands, and a cemetery with chain-link fence and the warning: GUARD DOG.

The United States, in its thinking and in its laws, still operated under the 1896 Supreme Court decision of *Plessy* v. *Ferguson*, which held: "We consider the underlying fallacy of the plaintiff's argument to consist in the assumption that the enforced separation of the two races stamps the colored race with a badge of inferiority. . . . The argument also assumes that social prejudices may be overcome by legislation, and that equal rights cannot be secured to the Negro except by an enforced commingling of the two races. We cannot accept this proposition. If the two races are to meet on terms of social equality, it must be the result of natural affinities, a mutual appreciation of each other's merits and a voluntary consent of individuals. . . . 'This end can neither be accomplished nor promoted by laws which conflict with the general sentiment of the community upon whom they are designed to operate . . .' Legislation is powerless to eradicate racial instincts or to abolish distinctions based upon physical differences, and the attempt to do so can only result in accentuating the difficulties of the present situation. If one race be inferior to the other socially, the Constitution of the United States cannot put them upon the same plane."

In May of 1918, John Ed Patten, thirty-nine years old, out of the church and the restaurant business, had set himself up in a candy store on San Felipe Street, one of the main thoroughfares of the Fourth Ward. The business had begun to prosper, and he gave it most of his waking hours, sleeping many nights in the back of the store to keep an eye on his merchandise.

One night late, clearing his cash register, he was startled by a man who came into the shop and made a swipe at the money on the counter. Outraged, John Ed ran into the street after him, cursing, not sure what or how much had been stolen.

Coming back out of a café where his thief had disappeared, he heard a voice shout: "Catch that nigger; he's got a gun."

Too late he found, in the ensuing shots, that his apprehender was a white policeman.

Indicted by a grand jury for assault with intent to murder, he was brought to trial. The case and subsequent appeals of John Ed Patten reflected all the racial biases of the times.

Sitting with a bandaged hand in the courtroom, defended by a lawyer he did not know, John Ed gave his version of what happened:

"My name is John Patten. I live at 513½ San Felipe Street and have lived in Houston off and on for twenty-five years. I was born and raised in Evergreen, San Jacinto County, Texas. I am a confectioner. Have a family, wife and three children and myself. I have never been convicted of a felony in this, or any other state. I know what I am charged with now, shooting this officer, and it happened this way.

"I was fixing to close up about eleven or twelve o'clock and it seemed to me like someone was calling on the outside, and he come in to get some change, and I had my money on the counter, and he snatched something and run, but I don't know what it was, and I run out after him and followed him to the restaurant, and I went in there, and I started across the street and stumbled and fell, and I heard somebody say, 'Catch that nigger; he has got a gun,' and I turned on Heiner Street, and as I turned, somebody was shooting at me, one or two people, and as I got to the corner of Heiner and Saulnier, I threw up my hands to surrender, and that is the time I got shot through the hand . . . and that is the time I shot at the officer. I am right-handed and had the pistol in the same hand I picked it up off the ground, the right hand. At the time I was shot through the hand I had my hands up, surrendered, and at that time I got shot through here and I got excited, and that is the time I must have shot. I surrendered and got shot through the hand. And after that, they came to my house and arrested me . . ."

On cross-examination by District Attorney John Crooker he repeated the same version, more frantic, conveying both the fear that had operated that night and the fear that had returned before the impassive all-white jury:

"I was in my place about midnight, or something like that, and the door was open and somebody came in there and asked for change. I had one light burning. I don't know who that was, he was a colored man, but I don't know who he was. Can't tell whether a tall man or a short man, didn't pay any attention to his size; don't know whether he had on a coat, or in his shirt sleeves, and don't know whether he had a hat on or not. It was just a Negro man and that is all the description I can give. He seemed to have taken some of my money, but I am not quite certain about that; he made a rake at something. I don't know how much he took, would not swear he took any, but he made an effort to take some, and then I got my gun and ran him as far as the restaurant. I got the gun from the back room, the sleeping room. When I got to the door he was about at the corner of Fuller Street and I ran after him pretty fast, and I went in the restaurant which is about the middle of the next block. . . I did not find the Negro that took the money, nor any trace of him. I had been drinking a little bit, been drinking some gin. I came on back down the street with the pistol in my pocket. I had gone up to the restaurant and went in and then came out of the restaurant and stopped just as I got out of the door. I stumbled across the streetcar track, and someone hollered, 'Catch that nigger; he has a gun' . . . And I picked up the gun and run. They got after me and I ran up San Felipe to Heiner and turned on Heiner and they commenced shooting as soon as I turned the corner, and I got down in the dark, and when I got to the corner I threw up my hands and surrendered . . . I do not remember shooting . . . I was so excited when they shot my hand I don't know what I did . . ."

The policeman testifying to his version conveyed, most of all, an outrage that his person had been shot at by a black; that such a thing could be allowed to take place seemed cause enough for conviction.

"My name is W. J. Riney and I am a police officer of the City of Houston, and have been for the past six months . . . I was on duty as a police officer in the Fourth Ward, San Felipe District. That is a Negro district almost exclu-

sively, it is considered a Negro district. I was on duty with
Officer Hight; he and I were partners working together.
One officer works in other parts of town, but they work
two out there. All ward beats work two men . . . We
were working from eleven at night until seven in the
morning. As alleged in the indictment, this defendant made
an assault upon me with the intent to kill me . . . He
shot at me twice before I shot at him . . . I couldn't see
him, it was so dark, but there was an arc light to my back
and he could get a good view of me. He was in the dark
and the light was behind me. I got within about fifteen feet
of him and he turns and said, 'Stop, you white son-of-a-
bitch,' and at the same time cut down on me. I mean he
shot at me with his pistol, and the first shot went right in
here and is still in me. This coat is the same coat I had on
that night, and the bullet went through where this hole is
in the coat. The bullet went in from the outside of the coat
to the inside, and entered right over the right nipple. It
went straight in and is in there now. I don't know how far
in it is. They probed for it twice and couldn't locate it. At
the time the first one hit me I turned my shoulder to him
and the second one cut the second button off my coat, and
the third shot went through here. The second shot cut this
button off, and this button I have pulled out of my pocket
is the one the second shot hit . . . The third shot entered
here, in the left-hand side of my coat lapel, at the point
where the coat is closed, pretty close to the heart . . .

"I couldn't say which side of Heiner Street he was on
when he stopped and applied this epithet to me and began
shooting. I claim that I shot only twice, and that this darky
shot six times . . ."

Hight, his partner, tried to substantiate his story, but had
apparently seen nothing very clearly. "Riney was closer to

him than I was. He was a hundred feet closer to him than I was; they were running fast, and I wasn't. I am stouter, and I wasn't doing my best because I thought he would go into one of those places. I knew that I could not outrun him. He was a Negro, and I knew from my experience that I could not outrun one of them. I did not see who fired the first shot . . . I fired two shots myself. I fired two shots and the darky was running . . . It was shortly after midnight when this thing occurred, and we both had our uniforms on. We had new uniforms, too."

The defense called in a doctor to testify that the shot in Patten's hand had entered through the palm, and that therefore he must have had his hands up in a gesture of surrender, as he claimed, when he was wounded. White shopkeepers in the neighborhood of the confectionery were called in as character witnesses:

"My name is L. Sonnen, and I run a grocery and meat market out on San Felipe. I have not lived in this country all my life, but have lived in it for forty-six years. I know the defendant John Patten, have known him for a little over seven years. I know the defendant's reputation in the community; so far as I know, he has been peaceable . . . I know a good many people out there where this Negro lives, and I should judge I know about seventy per cent of the same people he knows. I have never heard anything against his character."

"My name is M. Chira . . . I live at 1010 Heiner Street, and have lived in this country for twenty years. I know the defendant and have known him about nine years . . . I know the defendant's general reputation in the community in which he lives for being a peaceable, law-abiding Negro . . ."

However, S. B. Ehrenwerth, the lawyer representing

Patten, failed to call two eyewitnesses who had been sub-
poenaed and who were in the courtroom at the time. Later
he claimed that they had been frightened and did not wish
to get in trouble with the police. Later they claimed that
no one had asked them to tell what they had seen.

When the evidence was in, the presiding judge of the
Criminal District Court of Harris County instructed the
jury: "That you may understand the nature of the offense
with which the defendant is charged, it is necessary that
the Court define to you the offense of assault and of
murder. The use of any unlawful violence upon the person
of another with intent to injure him, whatever be the
means or degree of violence used, is an assault . . . Every
person with sound memory and discretion who, with mal-
ice aforethought, shall unlawfully kill any person, within
this state, shall be guilty of murder. Murder is distinguished from every other species of homicide by the absence of circumstances which reduce the offense to negli-
gent homicide or manslaughter or which excuse or justify
the homicide . . ."

He made no mention of the defendant's right to defend
himself against assault with a deadly weapon; or that under
those circumstances, even if the policeman had been killed,
the most severe penalty would have been manslaughter,
which would probably have been probated because Patten
had never committed a felony; or that since Riney had
lived, the only possible charge against Patten could be assault and battery.

The all-white jury responded as expected to the black
man who had fired at a white officer: It declared him
guilty as charged. The judge handed down a devastating
sentence: "It is, therefore, considered and adjudged by the
Court that the defendant John Patten . . . be punished, as

has been determined, by confinement in the penitentiary for ten years."

Panicked, John Ed raged at his attorney. Why hadn't he called the eyewitnesses who had sat throughout the trial in the back of the courtroom? Why hadn't he pointed out that there was no possible way he could be guilty of intent to murder, when all he had intended was to get out of the thing alive? Would he appeal?

Intimidated, Ehrenwerth backed down. There was nothing to be done. He washed his hands of the case. It was a lost cause.

Feverishly, John Ed secured another, black, attorney, J. M. Gibson, who worked around the clock to present, the next day, a motion for a new trial. When that did not succeed, he got his client out on bail of five thousand dollars—put up by the white shopkeepers—so that he could support his family while litigation pended, and appealed the case directly to the Court of Criminal Appeals in Austin.

Pointing out in his brief that the attorney now representing appellant was not the attorney who appeared at the trial, Gibson raised those matters which had been prejudicial to Patten's case in the lower court's proceedings: that the judge had not charged the jury correctly, that the all-white jurors were racially biased, that witnesses present in the courtroom had not been called.

But the state court in Austin did not consider that any point of law prevailed to alter the original decision from Harris County, and, on February 12, 1919, affirmed the lower court's judgment.

In one last, frantic appeal, Gibson pleaded: "The writer with some hesitation requests the Court, in view of its heavy docket, to again review the evidence in this case, but feels it his duty to do so. The statement of the evidence given in the Court's opinion in the main is correct but certain important details seem to have escaped notice . . . Now, here was an excited Negro in a dimly lit street after midnight . . . This court ought to judicially know from records appealed from Harris County, Texas, that the police of Houston, when a Negro runs from them, immediately begin shooting . . ."

But all avenues of mitigation had closed to him, and the defendant was sent to the penitentiary. If the policeman had succeeded in killing him, or if he had killed the policeman and been lynched, he would never have stood trial. As it happened, by the thinnest of accidents in the dark, John Ed Patten had survived to serve his sentence.

Huntsville State Penitentiary at that time was barbarous and brutal incarceration. It was a question of surviving, not of rehabilitation. Daily, prisoners were transported to work the fields in cages mounted on flatbed trucks, shackled together by "black nellies"—metal chokers attached to chains. Guards whipped them with bridle rings, bullwhips, blackjacks, and leather bats. Instructed to cease if they drew blood, they seldom did. Mutilations were common: inmates cut their own tendons or cut off their hands as a protest against brutality.

Vermin and rodents crawled the tanks that served as cells, and the mess hall. Food was uniformly scant and ill-prepared. The daily fare consisted of beans, peas, sow belly, cornbread with weevils. Meat depended on any game that could be caught and killed and a cook bribed to prepare: jackrabbits, armadillos, squirrels.

Enduring this life, John Ed had also to endure the news that, in his absence, his small son had died of malnutrition.

Sent to prison on an inappropriately harsh sentence because of the prejudicial climate of the state, he got out after six years because of a political backlash against those very biases.

In 1917, Governor James E. Ferguson, opponent of Prohibition and friend of the tenant farmer, was impeached in a special session of the Texas Legislature. In 1925, barred from holding office again, he put his wife, Miriam "Ma" Ferguson, forward as a candidate. Running on a liberal platform, she adamantly opposed the secret Ku Klux Klan. Elected, her first act was a record number of pardons for black convicts.

John Ed Patten was among those released—on "full and unconditional pardon," "friendless and penniless," in the language of the law—into the custody of his faithful attorney, J. M. Gibson.

A free man, he enclosed himself in a fenced business, which was both a buffer against the world and an eyesore to it.

What future hopes he had, he now put on his eldest daughter, Arlyne, a bright girl already beginning to make a name for herself as an orator in the Baptist Church. As she grew up he encouraged her, built up her command of English, shaped her flare and fire with his inflections and intonations. Then, she, too, was lost to him.

Eschewing her considerable gifts, she chose instead to secure the middle-class respectable family life of which his prison term had robbed her. She married the catch of the church, handsome Tuskegee student Ben Jordan, and put her past, good and bad, out of her life.

Outraged, robbed again of promise, John Ed refused to attend his daughter's wedding. Instead, he marked his days by the pound and the dollar as he watched her turn her full attention to being Ben's subservient wife, and the mother, in four years, of three daughters.

He was a man of fifty-seven, straight, spectacled, lonely, when he received into his arms his youngest granddaughter.

Barbara Charline, born February 21, 1936, was nurtured and welcomed by her mother, as finances had improved enough that Arlyne did not have to suffer confinement at Jeff Davis Charity Hospital, but could pay their cousin, Dr. Thelma Patten, to deliver the child at home; her father, on the other hand, looked at this third female, coalblack and glistening, and asked "Why is she so dark?"

This obstreperous infant's immediate response to him gave John Ed one last chance. By the time she was ten months old, he carried around a snapshot of her marked: MY HEART.

Here was someone at last to whom he could give all the lessons he had learned. He gave her the money and meat which you did not have if you were poor or behind bars. He gave her a God who did not say bend your knee and await a better day. He gave her autonomy, telling her, "Do not take a boss. Do not marry. Look at your mother." He gave her his guarantee that he would always be there when she needed him.

He read to her in the front bedroom of the frame house at Webster and Matthew streets, across from the Oliver Neon Company, a few blocks from the Good Hope Missionary Baptist Church, which he refused to attend; read to an attentive, skinny, long-legged five-year-old, with hair in tight plaits, her face fastened on his; read rocking back and forth in an old chair stuffed with cushions, peering over his dime-store, wire-rimmed reading glasses, by the light of a kerosene lantern, from a worn volume of *Songs for the Blood Washed:*

> I take the narrow way
> I take the narrow way
> With the resolute few who dare go through
> I take the narrow way
>
> I leave the world behind
> After the Lord to go
> Renouncing with a steadfast mind
> Its pride, and pomp, and show.
> No cumbrous garb I wear
> My progress to impede
> My pilgrim robe, divinely fair
> Is fashioned for all speed.
>
> I cannot slack my pace
> For earth's fantastic show;
> For like a flint I've set my face
> That I'll to Zion go.

He read from the King James Bible, and from Saalfield's Standard Vest Pocket Webster's Pronouncing Dictionary.

He talked to her as a teacher to a student, as a guide to a traveler, as an aging man to what had become the idol of his life—allowing him to become the foundation, the cornerstone, of hers.

In time, when she was at college, set on a path of becoming the Washington lawyer of a new generation, he found no further use for himself.

One evening, drunk on wine, wandering aimlessly, he stumbled on the railroad tracks and was hit by a train, which severed both his legs at the hips.

"Don't let Barbara see me," he begged Arlyne.

"What are you doing here?" he asked his favorite when she arrived at Jeff Davis Hospital to stare down at the spot where the sheet dropped flat.

Seeing her one last time, he gave in and died—abdicating a world which had left him without a leg to stand on.

■

2. THE JORDANS

Now, the thing of super importance in our life at my Grandfather Jordan's house, where we lived, was the Good Hope Missionary Baptist Church.

Sunday morning was a time of much activity in that household because everybody had to get ready and we had to be at Sunday school; and there was never any discussion about whether you would go, you just always had to go.

First we had a prayer service in the kitchen by the gas stove, all of us bowing our heads in a semicircle, and then we climbed into the two cars we had at the time—Grandfather Charles Jordan's Model T, and my father's old black Olds—and went to church.

The first person you saw in Good Hope was my grandfather, Charles Jordan, because he was the chairman of the deacon board and he had to be there promptly to open the service. He sat on one side of the table in front of the pulpit—below a picture of his wife's father, who was a former pastor of Good Hope—waiting to lead the opening hymn.

He gave it out in words and the congregation repeated it in singing. "I love the Lord, He heard my cry," my grandfather would say, and then the congregation would pick it up. After that there was a scripture reading and a prayer. When it was my grandfather's turn to pray, he would be sure to give the pastor, Reverend Lucas, a special mention and Good Hope a special mention, and then, when he was winding up his prayer, he would ask Jesus to ride for us. He'd say: "Ride on!" And then he would list all the places where he wanted Jesus to ride. Ride in the streets and ride in the homes and ride in the schools. "Ride on, Jesus!" He would be on his knees in front of that church, and it just seemed to me that if Jesus failed to ride he would be doing us a disservice.

After this there would be a prelude by Miss Mattie Thomas, who was the organist, and then anyone who had ever been a minister in his life would walk out from the back and sit up behind the pulpit, and then the choir would sing. And at that time my father was in the tenor section.

Bennie and Rose Mary were with the little penny-collection girls in blue capes who came out at a set time and sat on the third row of center aisle. They took up one of the three offertories that took place at Good Hope. My Grandmother Jordan was always at one end of the second row, and at the opposite end of the same row was my Grandmother Patten. Those were the seats they would sit in every Sunday of their lives. And my mother had a place, and she was very uncomfortable if she did not get that seat. And I sat with my mother in the audience. So everybody had a place.

Now my mother always carried a handkerchief which matched her outfit, and that was the way it was supposed to be, that was all a part of the program of action for her at church, because she always had an enormous pride in the way she looked. And at the time the minister got up to talk and preach, she would take this handkerchief out of her purse and spread it on her left knee for me to rest my head on because I was going to sleep—it was understood that I was going to sleep—and she didn't want the Excellento from my hair to get on her dress.

Then when the preacher got to the windup of his sermon, which my father used to always call the Exegies, when he got to the loud part of it, I would wake up. That's because the people would start shouting, and usually the manner in which to guarantee a shout, then as now, was for the preacher to put Jesus on the cross dying for our sins. At that, the congregation would scream and shout. They would let it all out and cry and yell. They might say: "Jesus!" They might say: "Hallelujah!" They might say: "Lord, help me!" But they would shout and it was very loud.

Now, one day it came time that I had to join that church. I had promised my Grandpa Patten that I would wait to join until I was twelve, because that was the age that Jesus was when he went into the temple. But there got to be too much pressure. At my Grandmother Patten's house the kids in the neighborhood played games outside, and their main game was one in which the sinners were separated from the Christians. And when the separation time came my sisters could join the Christians, but I could not, because I had not joined church. So I got tired of being a sinner in those games. And I decided to bring that to a halt.

I did not tell my mother that I was planning to join church on the Sunday I did. After the sermon, during the invitational hymn, when the minister opened the doors of the church to the unsaved, and I got up to go down front, I could hear my mother saying: "Where is she going?"

I gave Brother Lucas my hand and he told me to have a seat in one of the chairs placed in the front of the church, where I was in the care of the church clerk, Miss Marie, who took my name and put it on a card.

Then at the conclusion of the hymn, Reverend Lucas gave Miss Marie a nod to tell her it was time to say who was joining the church, and she stood up and said: "We have a little Sister as a candidate for baptism. We have a little Sister, Barbara Jordan." Then Reverend Lucas turned around to the choir and said to my father: "Ben, I think this is the last button on your coat." And my father was there grinning, just going: "Yeah, yeah." And Reverend Lucas said: "All right, Barb"—he always called me Barb— "make your statement." And I said, "I want to join church, to be baptized, and become a Christian." So, fine, someone offered a motion that the little Sister become a candidate for baptism.

On the first Sunday night of the next month, when it was time for the baptism, I was taken by my mother to a basement dressing room, where some ladies had a white sheet and a swimming cap for me. When I was all dressed in whatever I had to have on, I came up. They had pushed back the picture of John baptizing Jesus in the river Jordan to reveal the baptismal pool behind the choir, and there, sitting on the edge of this pool with his feet in the choir section, was my Grandfather Jordan. And, in front of him, the Reverend Lucas in tall rubber boots and a black robe.

Now, I was a little frightened of the water because it was a big pool, more water than I had ever been in. But I walked down the three steps into the pool, and over to Reverend Lucas, who turned me around, put his left hand on my shoulder, and, holding up his other hand, said: "In obedience to the Great Head of the Church, I baptize you, My Sister, in water."

At that point he put his right hand over my nose and down I went, backwards. Immediately after he brought me up, my Grandfather Jordan, who was still sitting on the edge, commenced to sing: "Wade in the water, children, wade in the water. God's going to trouble the water." Then I was taken downstairs and dried off, and my clothes were put back on so that I could go up into the auditorium. And there, to the delight of my head-deacon grandfather, I was extended the right hand of fellowship in Good Hope Missionary Baptist Church.

■

Barbara's parents met at Good Hope. Her mother Arlyne, the eldest daughter of John Ed Patten, had made a reputation for herself as an orator throughout the Baptist Church. "If Arlyne was going to speak, you knew you were well taken care of." "She was the speaker de luxe." "She was the most eloquent, articulate person I ever heard; if she'd been a man she would have been a preacher."

Her specialty was the welcoming address for state, district, and national Baptist conventions. "I wrote those speeches myself. I would search around and read up on the kind of books that gave examples of the different types of speeches, and then I would add a little something of my own to it. I liked doing that at the time." "At the time" being before her marriage, before her talent for oratory was submerged into mothering, ambition transferred, remaining only as a golden voice talking to babies.

Just out of high school in the early thirties, Arlyne was doing "day's work" for white families, and, at night, taking typing classes in the hope of bettering herself as a secretary, and, briefly, piano lessons in order to read music well enough to sing in the Gospel Chorus at Good Hope.

Barbara's father, Ben Jordan, grew up in Edna, Texas, a bright son for whom his family had high hopes. His mother, Mary, a Baptist missionary, urged him to attend Tuskegee, the Negro college in Alabama founded on the premise of separation by Booker T. Washington who, in his famous "hand speech," convinced his benefactors that educated blacks and whites could be like the fingers on the hand: all separate, able to work together. At the time Ben enrolled, Tuskegee was an almost legendary school for black Texans, the ultimate aspiration.

In his last year of college, however, Ben had to leave; times got harder, the dollar got scarcer, and his mother fell ill and could no longer work. He did not complete his degree, or play his last year of football.

Returning to Houston where his parents had settled, he got a job at the Houston Terminal Warehouse and Cold Storage and joined Good Hope. There he sang in the Junior Male Quartet and the Senior Choir, and there, inevitably, the prepossessing newcomer attracted the attention of the star of the young people, Arlyne Patten.

When Ben's mother died, he went in with his father on the purchase of a brick home on a newly paved street, with city sewers, electricity, and gas. Set on a rise of land northeast of town in the Fifth Ward, the neighborhood had fenced yards green with catalpa, willow, pecan, peach, plum, flowering oleander, and persimmon; and sidewalked front lawns trimmed with clipped boxwood hedges and pruned cedar shrubs.

Two years later, his father, Charles Jordan, was married a second time, to a woman named Alice Reed, a high school English teacher with a master's degree from Prairie View and doctoral credits earned summers in Colorado. The next year, Ben brought his own bride, Arlyne, home to the pink-trimmed house on Sharon Street.

At the time when Barbara was riding her three bicycles each in turn and awaiting Sundays with her Grandpa Patten, her sisters, Rose Mary and Bennie, were building relationships with the adults special to their own lives. For, as is always the case, no child has the same environment as do her siblings.

For Rose Mary, the eldest, church and home inevitably constituted a set of prohibitions.

Tall, thin, handsome, resembling her father in looks and manner, she spent her girlhood trying to please that stern, exacting man. He expected her to excel in school, to make A's, not B's. He assumed from the beginning that she would go to college—because *he* had. Later, when she began to date, he waited at the door at curfew time, not giving her a key, making her knock on the door so he would be sure to know when and in what condition she came in.

Rose Mary recounted: "We called him unusually strict. No movies, no dancing, no nothing. He never struck us, but the way he talked to us when he was displeased was more of a punishment than Mother's spankings. Just to have him question you frightened you to the point of never doing it again."

She hesitated. "Most of the time I felt he was quite

pleased with me. Periodically he would bring little items to me and we would converse about them. He was insistent with me that after my education I get a good job.

"Daddy was a religious man. Even before the call to the ministry he had been on the deacon board and president of the choir. After his call he devoted even more time to Bible study, meeting twice a week at night in a class of young ministers. He felt he had a message to give to the people.

"I got a lot of that from him. Sunday morning we had worship around the kitchen table, and he or my Grandfather Jordan said the prayer and we could volunteer to read the scripture, and I remember doing that a number of times because he always wanted us to. It carried over; at Good Hope I did Bible drills and Baptist Young People's Union and vacation Bible school, and at one point I could rattle off all the books of the Bible in a matter of seconds."

As is often the case with achieving eldest daughters who pattern themselves after their fathers, Rose Mary found it hard to select a female model. Her mother's family-centered hard work appeared in a negative light financially and intellectually. Of her life on Sharon Street, Rose Mary focused again on those things which were not allowed: "We were instructed not to go into other people's houses. There was a mulberry tree down the street and we were told not to eat the green berries because we would get worms. All the kids loved to pick blackberries, but Mother didn't want us to eat them because they had 'snake spit' on them."

The one woman she could take positive values from was her devout churchgoing grandmother, Martha Patten, a woman who had shown that neither bad times, nor lack of money, could keep her from being at Good Hope "when it opened, and being there when it closed at night." Rose Mary emulated her in the years of growing up. "My wanting to be involved with church affairs grew in part from 'Mama's' involvement. She instilled in me a principle that stayed with me. Being the eldest, I was the closest to her, and allowed to stay with her more, in the summers during vacation. If I got up early, she would let me think I was having coffee with her, though it would really be warm milk with the taste of coffee in it. They even tell me I favor her—"

This grandmother was also strict in ways that felt right to Rose Mary: she insisted on combing the girls' thick hair down to the roots no matter how it hurt, whereas their mother only worked the surface. She punished them with words when they deserved it.

For this daughter, through father and maternal grandmother, family and church instructions merged into a single message, one that could well have been taken from the words of the Baptist Covenant:

". . . [We engage] to seek the salvation of our kindred and acquaintances; to walk circumspectly in the world; to be just in our dealings; faithful in our engagements, and exemplary in our deportment; to avoid all tattling, backbiting, and excessive anger; to abstain from the sale of and use of intoxicating drinks and beverages; and to be zealous in our efforts to advance the kingdom of our Savior . . . "

Bennie, the middle daughter, led a wholly different life. Freed from the expectations placed on the eldest and the hopes clinging to the youngest, she took all that was warm and rich and sensuous from the households on Sharon Street and in the Fourth Ward.

She and Barbara, who filled out and blossomed early, were considered pretty girls, rounded, affectionate, sometimes mistaken for twins. She led her little sister by the hand, adored her, did the dishes for her when it was Barbara's turn, let Barbara sleep in the middle of the bed, taught her how to make friends and get along in school.

Bennie's memories of the Pattens are of "Mama" sitting on a kitchen stool with a big dishpan of pound-cake batter, letting them lick the metal spoon afterwards; of Sunday dinners replete with steaming greens, hot-water cornbread, gravied pot roasts, sweet-potato pie.

Her memories of Sharon Street are the fresh pine tree, cut for Christmas, which filled the house with fragrance. And music, always music. "At home on Sharon we sang the old gospels all the time. The piano was an upright, ting-a-ling type, but we played it all the time. I started picking out tunes that my stepgrandmother, whom we called 'Gar,' would play. I'd sit by her and watch what notes she hit and then play them back to her. We all sang and made music on Sharon Street.

"Later, we all sang in choirs. Mother sang every other Sunday in the Gospel Chorus, and Daddy sang in the Quartet and also in the Senior Choir, which he was president of. Barbara and Rose Mary and I performed as the Jordan Sisters. We gave concerts at Good Hope and everybody would look forward to hear us sing. Rose Mary sang first soprano and I sang second and Barbara sang alto. Later, after Daddy got his own church, and Rose Mary was off at college, Barbara and I continued as The Jordan Sisters, joining with two women from Greater Pleasant Hill Church to become The Counts and Jordan Sisters. I played for the white-robed choir and the purple-robed choir at Good Hope all the way through Texas Southern University. Then, in high school, Aunt Mamie got me started seriously in voice."

This aunt, who became Bennie's example as well as her teacher, was Alice Reed's daughter by an earlier marriage. A beautiful, vibrant woman, Mamie Reed went from Prairie View College to the University of Iowa, then to Westminster Choir College in Princeton, and, later, when she had summers off from teaching, to voice workshops at Columbia University and the Fred Waring Clinic in Pennsylvania.

"Wherever there was singing," Mamie Reed Lee said, "I would be there. The only thing that fulfilled me was music. I guess everybody was influenced by it. I taught all three Jordan girls; all of them started singing because that was my area. I was a diction specialist and I insisted on that with them. I taught them that you have to memorize the words to each song because you've got to be able to paint a picture to whomever you're singing.

"My mother was very close to Bennie. She would always have Bennie beside her on the piano stool when she was home. They would bang away. My mother was not a proficient musician—we called her 'the bumper'—but she loved it. We all loved it."

Mamie had been linked with this family even before her mother married Charles Jordan, for, as a little girl, she had been left in the loving care of Martha Patten and her kitchen while her parents attended out-of-town conventions. So her images of both these homes—that Mama's was warm and fragrant with food, that Gar's was filled with song—underlay Bennie's perceptions of them.

However different growing up at that time was for each of her three daughters, Arlyne found life in the house on Sharon Street a struggle. While her husband lent money for interest to his coworkers, frugally kept the two families in the crowded house, and in all ways executed the tight economies of a man who did not like to spend a nickel, Arlyne seized what autonomy she could.

Weekdays, at least, her mother-in-law was gone to a nearby town to teach and she had the kitchen to herself; weekends she got up before Gar to cook for her own family.

When Barbara was a toddler, Arlyne took the bus to town, not being able to drive, and got herself fitted for a diaphragm at the Planned Parenthood Center, deciding that three children born in four years were enough to raise.

What money she had—gifts from Ben, money made selling Christmas cards at church, and doing day work—she put into clothes for herself and her girls. No one must say that they were not as well dressed as anyone in church, that she had not married a fine provider, that they were not as good as anyone.

She made her own things look fine by co-ordinating hats and handkerchiefs with every outfit, as hats were cheaper than dresses when you had someone to make them for you. A prize outfit was a gray velour hat with round crown dressed with white feathers, a matching gray-and-aqua suit, gray shoes and bag, and a gray-and-aqua handkerchief; later it was a rust bonnet with cream satin trim to match a rust coat-dress with cream blouse, and cream handkerchief. These accessories, her prize possessions, stored in millinery boxes and plastic bags, were saved and rotated every season.

The pinnacle of her public presentation of the children was the year of the gabardine suits. Taking the bus to town to select material for the seamstress to make into Easter finery for her daughters, Arlyne fell in love with bolts of lavish pastel fabric, an expensive gabardine which required dry cleaning. Selecting a blue for Rose Mary, an aqua for Bennie, and her special pink for the baby, Barbara, she had these fashioned into the latest style: three-button jackets and flared skirts.

On the Saturday before Easter, as every Saturday, while the family took their baths, the little girls bathing together so as not to congest the hurried Sunday morning, Arlyne hung the new suits in the dining room, putting in three neat piles beneath them their new panties, clean white socks, and polished shoes.

Then Sunday morning, before the joint family gathered around the kitchen table for the scripture and prayer which preceded the three hours of hallelujah at church, she lined her daughters up in a row, pulled up kitchen chairs for them to sit on, and, heating the straightening iron, applied her homemade pressing oil of vaseline, oil of peppermint, and a "grower" to fix their hair.

Then, lined up tinted as Easter eggs in their fine suits, their hair pulled tight into three braids each, they stood in a row—awaiting candy eggs, the benediction of their father, and the risen Jesus.

The gabardine suits, and what they represented to Arlyne, was important enough that—for the only time in her daughters' memory—she raised her voice to Ben.

When, after a few weeks the suits needed refurbishing, she got on the bus and took them to be cleaned and pressed. When he found this out and railed at the cost, asking, "How do you think we can afford to dry clean children's clothes?", she rose on tiptoe to inform him: "I wanted the little girls to look nice, so I got them these suits. Now I've taken them to the cleaner's, and if you don't want to pay to get them out, they can just stay there."

The bill for the Sunday suits was paid.

It must have been two or three years after I was baptized that my father got up and acknowledged to the congregation that he had been called to preach. They have to go through a lot of experiences before they know that it is a genuine call that is being sent, so he had done that. He had doubted, and he had tried drinking, and he had hit a man with his car. He said he had done what he could to run away, but that God had called him. And when he first stood up in Good Hope and said he had been called to preach, I was confused. I didn't know what that meant. At first it struck me as sort of strange, because at this point the only person that I felt was qualified to preach was the Reverend Lucas, and I had difficulty seeing my father in this role.

But the preacher was very approving and he told my father that he would schedule his first sermon in the near future. These initial sermons were not held on Sunday mornings, but were given at a special time in the education building.

So one fine night we all went out to Good Hope, where my father preached his first sermon. I remember the text exactly. It was from Philippians, and it went: "I press toward the mark for the prize of the high calling of God in Christ Jesus." "I press toward the mark"—I liked that. That seemed an appropriate subject for someone giving a first sermon who says he's been called to preach. And my father, in acknowledging this call, preached a sermon about this call being an extension, a fulfillment of Christ in him, just as whatever we all do is supposed to be in response to what God wants. And as I sat there, I recall listening very carefully to try to figure out what he was saying, registering the fact that he was up there preaching, so that it must mean he was someone special. Which made those words stick in my mind. And I decided he was saying that God is subject to issuing a call to anybody—to him, to me, to anybody—and that what you have to do, if God calls you, is whatever He is telling you to do.

Then he became pastor of a church of his own—in the Houston Heights, which was kind of an old neighborhood —called Greater Pleasant Hill Baptist Church. So he had this old church, and it was a small church—and when I say small, I guess there were a dozen members—and I was accustomed to lots of people being in church. And here was a little church.

Well, needless to say, my father took all of us out there and mandated that we become members. Well, of course, Mother was willing; she knew that she had to do it. But I couldn't understand why we had to do it, Bennie and Rose Mary and I. I really had difficulty getting ready for that. But I didn't have half as much difficulty as Rose Mary. She cried all day because she didn't want to leave Good Hope. But it was about time for Rose Mary to go to Prairie View College, and I recall telling her: "Well, you'll be gone soon." I didn't cry, but I just know that I didn't think that church needed my attendance.

So one night my father announced to us: "Tonight all of you will join Greater Pleasant Hill." And I thought: "Why do we have to do that?" I recall saying to Bennie that night: "What do you think would happen if we just refuse to get up? He couldn't come down and bodily drag us up there. What if we just sat?" But that was out of the question at that time.

This was a one-family church, the Greater Pleasant Hill. The membership began with Deacon Counts and his wife, Mrs. Counts, and his two daughters, Odessa and Lillian, who were closer to my mother's age than to Bennie's and mine. The two of them would sing duets, and they asked if Bennie and I would join them, and we did—and we became The Counts and Jordan Sisters. Bennie would play for us, and we would schedule programs at various churches and offer to do a recital for them and negotiate so the terms would be fifty-fifty, half the money to the group and half the money to the church. And there we were. The Counts thought we were much better singers than I ever thought we were.

But there we were, raising money. My lead song was "Old Landmark" ("Let's all go back to the Old Landmark"). I don't know what that was, the "Landmark"; but "Let's all go back" was the message.

On some occasions I did a recitation in that church. At that time I was doing a lot of that. I remember one poem by James Weldon Johnson that was a favorite:

And God stepped out on space,
And He looked around and said,
"I'm lonely—
I'll make me a world."

And far as the eye of God could see
Darkness covered everything,
Blacker than a hundred midnights
Down in a cypress swamp.

Then God smiled,
And the light broke,
And the darkness rolled up one side,
And the light stood shining on the other,
And God said, "*That's good!*"

Then God reached out and took the light in His hands,
And God rolled the light around in His hands,
Until He made the sun;
And He set that sun a-blazing in the heavens.
And the light that was left from making the sun
God gathered up in a shining ball
And flung against the darkness,
Spangling the night with the moon and stars.
Then down between
The darkness and the light
He hurled the world;
And God said, "*That's good!*"

. . . .

And God walked, and where He trod
His footsteps hollowed the valleys out
And bulged the mountains up

. . . .

Fishes and fowl
And beasts and birds
Swam the rivers and the seas,
Roamed the forests and the woods,
And split the air with their wings,
And God said, "*That's good!*"

Then God walked around,
And God looked around
On all that He had made.
He looked at His sun,
And He looked at His moon,
And He looked at His little stars;

He looked on His world
With all its living things,
And God said, "*I'm lonely still.*"

Then God sat down
On the side of a hill where He could think;
By a deep, wide river He sat down;
With His head in His hands,
God thought and thought,
Till He thought, "*I'll make me a man!*"

Up from the bed of the river
God scooped the clay;
And by the bank of the river
He kneeled Him down;
And there the great God Almighty,
Who lit the sun and fixed it in the sky,
Who flung the stars to the most far corner of the night,
Who rounded the earth in the middle of His hand—
This Great God,
Like a mammy bending over her baby,
Kneeled down in the dust
Toiling over a lump of clay
Till He shaped it in His own image;
Then into it He blew the breath of life,
And man became a living soul.
Amen. Amen.

That's how it ended: "Amen. Amen." I liked that. And
that was the poem I recited on about a thousand occasions
at that time. It was about twice that long, as I recall.

So we did it all at Pleasant Hill, because we had to. At
one point I was even a superintendent of the Sunday
school. But I did not always co-operate. My father at that
time had special evening meetings when members would
get up and tell their determination, tell what they were

going to continue to do for the Lord. These were called Speaking Meetings. It was an innovation of that church, and we were supposed to speak in Speaking Meetings. So at one point my father said to me: "I think it's time for you to pray in public." But I was ready for that. I prayed so softly that no one could hear a word I said. And that was the end of my being required to pray. "Yes, ma'am," I said to myself, "This is one you can handle."

Eventually we did get back to Good Hope. My father was called to another church, in Thompsons, Texas, and he got this call for two Sundays a month, first and third, and he went to Greater Pleasant Hill and said: "I'm going to accept this church on these Sundays." He was only getting paid for two Sundays anyway, although he had been preaching four. But Deacon Counts said: "The first and third are our pastoral Sundays, and we are entitled to them." Well, this created an irreconcilable conflict, so my father resigned from Greater Pleasant Hill Baptist Church. Later, a lot later, he did get a second church in Kendleton, Texas, so he was always on the highway, and my mother was always on the highway.

I recall we had to rejoin Good Hope. We all had to get up and rejoin. And Reverend Lucas said to my father: "Ben, you're not going to take away my chaps again. They are here to stay." For which I wanted to say: "Thank you."

But by that time I had totally lost my opportunity to avoid night services, or BYPU, or choir practice, or prayer meetings. So the evenings with my Grandfather Patten were gone. They were really over.

I do not recall joy related to my experience of these years at church. What I got from them was a charter, a

single plan offered to you that you must fulfill because that
was the only acceptable way:

> Only one life, it will soon be past;
> Only what's done for Christ will last.

How to die, we got that. But we were missing how to
live. I do not recall any message of joy or love or happiness
generated out of this experience. It was a confining, re-
stricting mandate. I did not feel free to do anything other
than what was being presented to me as the way one must
proceed; that whatever you do in this life has to be in
preparation for that other life. So, on balance, my church
relationship was, without doubt, a very imprisoning kind
of experience.

Home, in those years, reflected the same attitudes. It was
a very restrictive environment. There was a plan for our
behavior that did not take the present into account.

We lived with my Grandfather Jordan and his wife,
who was not my father's mother, because my father's
mother died and my grandfather married again. The seven
of us lived in a brick house which had been financed under
Franklin Roosevelt's Reconstruction Finance Corporation.
This house was my grandfather and my father's joint venture when neither of them was married, and my father felt
that, as he had made this contract with his father, he should
stay with us in that house.

And for a time it was all right—we had a paved street,
which was unusual then for black neighborhoods, and
there was a big juniper tree which I thought was beautiful
—but later as everybody started to grow up things got a little sticky. It was a two-bedroom house, with my grandfather and Gar occupying the front bedroom, and my par-

ents the little back one. The three of us slept on a foldout bed. And I would always sleep in the middle. (I wonder why. It seems to me, if Bennie were the middle child, she would have been in the middle, but that was not the case. Rose Mary would be on the outside, I would be in the middle, and Bennie would be next to the wall.)

At one point my father built an additional room, so that the three of us could move out of the dining room into the middle bedroom, and my mother and father took the new back room. We had one bathroom, and you just did the best you could to get in.

So there were seven of us in that house.

Grandfather Jordan was a big man in physical stature. He worked for the Southwestern Paper Company and drove a big red truck for them, and he'd bring it home sometimes to put in the driveway on Sharon Street. He sat on the front porch a lot and chatted with the neighbors who would come by to see the red truck. This grandfather was so jealous of my relationship with my Grandpa Patten he could hardly stand it. He'd come up to me with: "You like your grandfather Patten better than you like me?" Of course I did not answer that.

My stepgrandmother, Gar, taught school in the country, and when she came home on the weekends she usually talked nonstop about the school, the principal, the faculty, the students, the plans, the programs; and I would know the names of the principal of the school and the names of the other teachers if I didn't know anything else.

She always played the piano and Bennie was always at the piano with her—she was her favorite and she called her Benito. And Rose Mary was always reading *Little Women*. So I was always outside riding my bicycles, one at a time, up and down the sidewalk.

My father at that time was definitely not pleased with me. I remember that. We did not see eye to eye on anything. He felt called upon to brag to acquaintances about the excellence of his three girls. He would say: "I'm raising three girls in the heart of the city." (It wasn't.) "And they don't drink, they don't smoke, they don't dance, they don't play cards, they don't go to the movies. I tell you it's hard, friends, to do that with three young girls in the heart of the city." And that would just cause me the squeemies of the gut. I thought: "How can he go around bragging about the fact that he has three freaks?"

(We did go to a movie once; Mother sneaked us off. She didn't do it personally, but she allowed a cousin, who lived on Sharon Street also, to take us to the Lyons Avenue Theater to see Shirley Temple. That was a big thrill. It was a very exciting adventure.)

My father did not like my attitude concerning meat. I wanted to have meat at my meals; I felt that there had to be a separate serving of meat in order for the meal to be complete. Sometimes we would have fish, but my recollection of having fish is of Mother fixing each of our three plates, sitting there picking every bone out of the fish for us, while the three of us sat side by side at the red-and-white-checked tablecloth. I recall a lot of meals with rice and beans, baby lima beans or pinto beans, and greens, collard greens, and I did not like any of that. We would always have dessert, cake or pie—my mother made lemon pie, and she made blackberry cobbler, and peach cobbler; and homemade rolls we would have, the kind you make with yeast cake and let them rise under a damp dishcloth in the refrigerator. But no meat.

On several occasions my father said to me: "If you want some meat, you can go buy it." This was a reminder of who earned the money in that family. But I always had money from my Grandpa Patten, so I did buy some. I would bring home a serving of hot sausage, which I did not share with Bennie or Rose Mary.

There was also the incident of the coat. I very much wanted one of those heavy coats with the hood on them, and I asked my father for this and he said no, that he couldn't afford to buy one. So I went to Grandpa Patten and he bought it for me. Then one day I heard my father brag to another man about this beautiful coat that his little girl was wearing, and I piped up with: "You didn't buy it for me." And he was naturally embarrassed at being sassed back in front of the other man.

Then, of course, I was supposed to take piano lessons from Miss Mattie Thomas, because Bennie and Rose Mary had done that, and that is what you were expected to do. Miss Mattie would have these musical recitals once a year at Good Hope, with her students from the *Au Fait* music school, and she would cover the podium area with artificial green grass and rent a grand piano. And Bennie and Rose Mary and I did that in our long dresses. I took lessons for two years, but that was all of it. So one day I announced to Miss Mattie in front of the other students that I no longer wished to take piano. At which point she called my father to say she had been very embarrassed by my highhanded way. And of course he did not like that.

My father and I did not get on in those years.

Now, in terms of other relationships, Rose Mary was attached to our father, and Bennie and I were close to each other, but we were all close to our mother. We were with her all the time and she was working for us all the time. I really think the three of us were always close to her.

It was usually me who got in trouble with her, and she

would have to spank me with a leather belt. I would try to
wear her down and wear her out, but finally, if she didn't
get tired or laugh at the whole thing, I would fall on my
back on the floor and kick my feet in the air so that
Mother would get kicked if she tried to get close enough
with the belt. We did a lot of that.

But if I was not in trouble, I would come in from school
and sit down on the floor beside her to hear "Stella Dallas"
and "Portia Faces Life" and "Just Plain Bill"; the first
order of business in the afternoons after school was to hear
the latest radio episodes in the living room. They were just
members of my mother's family, and I liked that.

But mostly my mother was busy from dawn to dark
washing the clothes, ironing the clothes, fixing the meals,
and keeping the house. Washing involved heating the big
black tub in the back yard, and then, after you had heated
the big washtub with a lot of soap and stirred everything
with a stick until you had sudsy water, you had bleach
water, and you had a tub called bluing. And it took all of
my mother's time attending to these things. I guess I assumed that I would grow up and marry a man like my father and spend all of my time washing and pressing his
khakis, washing and pressing the children's clothes, and
making sure the children had breakfast and supper and that
my husband had all he wanted to eat when he got home.

I don't know that I ever thought: "How can I get out of
this?" I just know that there were some things that I did
not want to be a part of my life, but I had no alternatives
in mind at that point. Since I didn't see movies, and we
didn't have television, and I didn't go anyplace with anybody else, how could I know anything else to consider?

So I was as accepting of life then as I could manage, because I did not have a choice. It would have been fun to

rebel at some point, but I didn't. You just didn't. I had to be where I was because at that point in time I had to be taken care of by my parents. I knew there were some things that I wanted to be different for me at some later date, but most of the time I went along with the way things were.

I think that is an accurate picture of how it was at our house. I really do.

3. PHILLIS WHEATLEY HIGH SCHOOL

In 1949, when Ben had added his preacher's call to his warehouse job, and Rose Mary had gone off to Prairie View College, he and Arlyne at last moved out of the Jordan house into a residence of their own. The new Campbell Street frame house, painted the favorite pink, sat across the present freeway from the Sharon Street neighborhood on a rise of slash and loblolly pines, among schools, stores, churches, hospitals, and community centers.

The following year, the Supreme Court declined to reconsider the fifty-three-year-old doctrine of "separate but equal" established in *Plessy* v. *Ferguson*. The *Plessy* dispute involved an individual of "seven-eighths Caucasian and one-eighth African blood," who had been thrown in jail for sitting in a whites-only railroad coach in Louisiana. In 1896, only Justice John Marshall Harlan recognized that the issue was not one of "social" but of "civil" rights, that the dispute had nothing to do with equal accommodations but everything to do with equal standing before the law. In his dissenting opinion, Harlan had argued: "The white race deems itself to be the dominant race in this country. And so it is, in prestige, in achievements, in education, in wealth, and in power. So, I doubt not, it will continue to be for all time, if it remains true to its great heritage and holds fast to the principles of constitutional liberty. But in the view of the constitution, in the eyes of the law, there is in this country no superior, dominant, ruling class of citizens. There is no caste here. Our constitution is color blind, and neither knows nor tolerates classes among citizens. In respect of civil rights, all citizens are equal before the law . . . The arbitrary separation of citizens, on the basis of race . . . is a badge of servitude wholly inconsistent with the civil freedom and the equality before the law established in the constitution."

In 1950, *Sweatt* v. *Painter* gave the Supreme Court the opportunity to reconsider the "separate but equal" doctrine. The plaintiff was a black male student who had been refused admission to the University of Texas Law School on the grounds that substantially equivalent facilities were offered by the newly created one-room law school at Texas Southern University, the former Texas State University for Negroes, across the north-south viaduct from Campbell Street and the Fifth Ward.

Hedging the basic issue that separate cannot be equal, the Court held for Sweatt by finding the separate facilities unequal: ". . . [T]he University of Texas Law School possesses to a greater degree those qualities which are incapable of objective measurement but which make for greatness in a law school. Such qualities, to name but a few, include reputation of the faculty, experience of the administration, position and influence of the alumni, standing in the community, traditions and prestige. It is difficult to believe that one who had a free choice between these law schools would consider the question close . . .

"The law school to which Texas is willing to admit petitioner excludes from its student body members of the racial groups which number 85% of the population of the State and include most of the lawyers, witnesses, jurors, judges and other officials with whom petitioner will inevitably be dealing when he becomes a member of the Texas Bar. With such a substantial and significant segment of society excluded, we cannot conclude that the education offered petitioner is substantially equal to that which he would receive if admitted to the University of Texas Law School."

Heman Marion Sweatt, by then a weary man in his forties, was admitted to the law school in Austin, where he flunked out; and Texas Southern, the university whose law school had been created to keep him out, became a symbol of the judiciary's first admission that all-black institutions provided second-class educations for those who were still second-class citizens.

Teachers in high schools such as Phillis Wheatley—named for a famous black poet born in 1753 in Africa, who came as a slave to Boston and became a maidservant to the wife of John Wheatley—where the Jordan sisters went, had dealt with this fact for years, and fought it by whatever means they knew. One such teacher was Mamie Reed Lee, Ben's stepsister, who had dedicated herself to broadening the cultural advantages offered to segregated students. She recalled: "I spent a lot of time trying to give our black children cultural exposure they wouldn't otherwise have had. We took about one hundred and fifty kids a year in busloads to concerts and to the Houston Symphony. The parents paid the bus fee of a quarter and concert ticket of fifty cents.

"The biggest event was Marian Anderson. It was a big thing in all our lives to hear her, and, because at that time she came almost every year to stay with a family in Third Ward, we got to hear her often. As she had a policy against performing to segregated audiences, we accepted, in order to hear her, that if all the blacks were in the balcony that was probably because there were so many of us.

"I kept a picture of Marian Anderson on my wall at school. I used to play up her coming to Barbara, make a big do over the fact that she was a contralto, as Barbara was trying to be a contralto—at least I wanted her to. Barbara had the same gestures and mannerisms as Anderson, the same stately way to her walk. She was articulate and impressive in the same way. I thought Barbara could become someone like that if she wanted to."

But for students like Barbara, having no access to visible examples of parity, living adjacent to a black college in an area bounded by the limits of black housing, reading black newspapers, such experiences as Anderson could not furnish exit from their closed world. Without expectation of change, without anger, they continued to deal with the status quo.

Barbara debated integration at Phillis Wheatley; her notes from one debate reveal the acquiescence of the times:

"1. Talk of integration may seem out of place, but when one discovers the kind of difficulty to which such practices lead and weighs them against the values of unity, one can easily see why, even in a day of great diversification, the term 'integration' becomes a popular one.

"2. One must recognize at the outset that integration is a process whose end will probably not be fully realized in our generation. Yet, although we may not receive the victory, the quest is worth our effort.

"3. The effort in the direction of integration has always involved uprooting a preconceived notion of separation, as witness the slow progress of the Negro.

"4. While, to be sure, we are students in a segregated institution, and while certainly we must work within the framework of the laws of our state, let it be realized by every student that the challenge facing us is not the defense of any system, be it segregated or integrated; the challenge facing us is to so equip ourselves that we will be able to take our place wherever we are in the affairs of men. The sands of time are slowly running out and the funeral dirge will soon be heard. But there should be no weeping on our part, for we should welcome the day when we are no longer forced to live in a segregated and discriminated community.

"5. Ours should be a day of rejoicing for the privilege of being a man like other men, free to worship like other men, free to speak like other men, free to go to school like other men, free to get a job like other men.

"6. Our country is made up of a variety of groups and each should have its place. There is no cause for the continuation of segregation and discrimination which will always bring conflict and confusion. Harmony, so essential for our internal security and national defense, can be achieved through integration. To be sure, there will be many who will make an effort to impede progress in the direction of integration, but we must not be misled by their jabberings."

At Phillis Wheatley, Barbara dealt, as she always does, with the specifics of the moment. The matter at hand: to move past the prohibitions of home and church into the freewheeling world of peers, to go from bicycling around the block to learning the rules of school.

At first, this consisted of establishing the gang. "The school would close at three o'clock every day and the kids would gather at a particular place, there on Lyons Avenue. The kids being me, and Bennie, and two of the Justice sisters, Evelyn and Mary Elizabeth, and Charles White, and a couple of hangers-on.

"Charles White's family owned a grocery store there on Lyons, and he, also, always had some money in his pocket. I sort of envied Charles White's worldliness, because his family would go on trips, vacations, and none of us could do anything like that. You know when you're in school and you're out for the summer and you come back and everybody has to write a paper on 'How I Spent My Time over Vacation.' I can remember clearly that Charles White's family went someplace where he rode in a glass-bottom boat. And I thought: 'What a life, what a life.' And so he could talk about all of that, and of course, all I could talk about was how fast I could go on my bicycles. I really did have a little bit of envy of Charles White and his family's being able to send him on these exotic trips. I toyed with the idea of my lying about what I did, but I didn't know that I could pull that off. So I didn't.

"It would take us well over an hour to walk from Wheatley to Campbell Street, not because it was that far, but because we moved at a snail's pace. There was a store en route that sold hamburgers and hot dogs, and that was a regular stop. And Charles and I would buy for everyone. He and I were the leaders of the pack. And at that point I could share some of my larder with the group. Then we would stop and have sodas. My father had a soda-water business on Lyons Avenue, which he called Your City

Soda. He and a dentist had decided to go into business for the manufacture of orange and strawberry soda water to sell to local stores. So, after leaving the hamburger man, we would stop by Your City Soda and drink as much orange soda pop as we could. Then, after an epoch, we would be back in the street, inching along, and we would have this trek home from school. We would get from Lyons, where the school is located, to Solo Street, and then we would occupy the entire street, about ten or twelve of us strung across the street, and nothing could pass, car or bicycle, not anything, as we moved one step per five minutes en route down Solo until we got to Campbell. I thought this method of getting home was fine."

In high school, however, following Bennie's lead into a crowd of girls, Barbara received increasing pressure from home to "behave like a lady." Bored with the limited speed of her bicycle, she talked to her Grandpa Patten about putting a motor on her Schwinn and making it into a motorbike. He had instructed her to find out how that could be done. Calling Western Auto, she learned that converting to a motor would mean reinforcing the entire bicycle structure and would cost three hundred dollars. Grandpa said: "I guess I can do that." But Barbara's mother hit the ceiling. "Can't you see a girl on a motorbike with her skirt flying in the air?" And when Barbara reported this to her grandfather, he, sensing the way things were, went along. "I don't know if we can do this then, if your skirt is going to fly in the air." So the time of two-wheelers came to an end.

"I recall at this time that my worst grades were always in physical education, because I didn't want to put on the gym shorts and play the games any more. I was not riding my bikes at this time. I was interested in doing something else. So I didn't really bring a sense of dedication to succeeding in physical education classes."

Turning her mind to the world of the teen-age girl, she set out to follow what was popular. She wore the scoop-neck dresses and toeless pumps, the "gold" and rhinestone jewelry and smooth-bobbed pageboy of the rest. She wrote her favorite things in her yearbook: "EATS AND TREATS: Ice Cream, Champale, High Life, Fried Chicken; FAVORITE SINGERS: Mario Lanza, Dorothy Kirsten, Ivory Jo Hunter; FAVORITE MAGAZINE: *Seventeen;* FAVORITE DEEJAY: Dr. Daddy O; FAVORITE ACTRESS AND ACTOR: Hedy Lamarr and Victor Mature; FASHION FADS: The poodle cut and loud-colored shoes; SERIOUS AND FRIVOLOUS THOUGHT FOR THE FUTURE: To change Miss to Mrs. someday."

She learned to follow the team instead of lead it. "I was a very strong supporter of the football team. I wasn't a cheerleader, but I should have been. I felt I did a better job of leading the cheers than the cheerleaders. The big sports event in Houston, Texas, for all my high school years was the football game between Phillis Wheatley and Jack Yates, another black high school, in Third Ward. That game was a football classic; these schools were the two biggies. The rivalry was very intense. The rivalry between Fifth and Third Ward kids was intense anyway; Booker T. Washington, in Fourth Ward, where my mother graduated, was just not in the running. The game was always played on Thanksgiving Day at Jeppesen Stadium in Houston, and you would not be caught anywhere other than at the Wheatley-Yates game on that day.

"So it was load-up-the-car time and go to that game, and my father, who had played football at Tuskegee, approved of that. And he began to be pleased with me."

But most of all, she took her cues from Bennie. "The good thing about arriving at Wheatley was Bennie sort of paved the way for me. My Aunt Mamie was a teacher of music there, and Bennie and Rose Mary had been members of the All Girls' Choir, and one thing I really wanted to do was this All Girls' Choir.

"And Bennie and I were friends with Mary Elizabeth and Evelyn Justice who were neighbors on Campbell Street, and we had known them in elementary school, so we were just always together. In the evening Bennie and I and the Justices were always together, because, for one thing, I was the only one who could drive a car. I always wanted to drive some vehicle, so I took driver's education at Wheatley and got my license. Which you could do then at fourteen. I used my father's car, a dark-blue '49 Olds, and we would go to the Lincoln Drive-In and we'd have a hamburger and shake, not yet a beer in those days.

"(Later I got in trouble over cars, with my Grandfather Jordan's light-green '52 Olds, which Gar turned over to me when he died because she didn't drive. She left word with Mr. Greenwood at the Gulf service station that I could sign her name on gas tickets, but she thought I would only use the car for important trips. So my credit was cut off with Mr. Greenwood after two weeks. I really blew that one.)

"We were always together. At one point I said to my mother: 'I think I want to have a slumber party.' And she said: 'What is that?' And I said: 'Bennie and I will just get the Justices and everybody over here and we can stay up all night and just sleep on the floor.' So I had a slumber party. And we stayed up all night. It was not all right to go to sleep. So I did not do that.

"Bennie would make little sandwiches, or bake cakes. And we had cold drinks from Your City Soda. We'd talk about our ideas about boys, and other kids who seemed more advanced in their romantic life than we were, and we would wonder what it was like to really have a boy close to you, and we'd talk about sex a lot and not one of us knowing what we were talking about. Trying in an exploratory way to see how much each of us did know. We didn't talk about menstruation, pretended that did not exist, but I had learned of that from Rose Mary.

"And on one of these slumber-party occasions Rose Mary came back from Prairie View and she had stories that would just send your hair standing on end. She would tell us various experiences she had seen, passing on to all of us what things happened at college that you wouldn't believe.

"One thing: She said some of the girls smoked and they inhaled the smoke and some of them could even drink from a water glass and then exhale smoke rings. I said: 'I just don't believe it. We are going to have to try it.'

"So here we were about to have a class, with Rose Mary the teacher, in how to smoke a cigarette—Bennie and me and the Justices, on Campbell Street, for this daring, bold adventure.

"I bought the cigarettes, because I had this plaid jacket that I could put them in the pocket of. Pall Malls. I said that I was buying them for my father, and, you know, the guy at the grocery store knew that my father didn't smoke. When the demonstration time came I did not get choked; that is what I remember. I managed not to choke and cough, and I took about three swallows of water and blew smoke out, and I can't tell you what a grand event that was. And we just couldn't wait until we could go and do all those wild, exciting things that were happening in college.

"Another event at this time was Hester House. Mildred Brooks, the biology teacher at Wheatley, had a choral group called the Hester House Girls. And Bennie and I would sing in that. Hester House was about four blocks from Campbell Street, so we were members of the singing group and we could go down there, and that was acceptable.

"But on Friday night Hester House had a canteen and they would invite fellows from Ellington Field Air Base to come, and we could not go to that because there was dancing and that was not allowed. But from time to time we would sneak over to the Justices and we'd go anyway. The fellows from Ellington Air Force Base would come in the bus and they would all be deposited there.

"I would usually sing; I wasn't a very good dancer because I had never danced, as we were not allowed to. So I didn't want to get out there and make a fool of myself. But I felt comfortable singing, and I could get some of the latest numbers and render them. We would have a ball. My special favorite was called 'Money, Honey.' It went like this: 'The landlord rang the front doorbell; I let it ring for a long, long spell. I looked through the window, I peeped through the blind, and I asked him to tell me what was on his mind. He said, "Money, Honey."' That was my specialty.

"And the highlight of the evening would be if you were lucky enough to catch one of the airmen and have the bus parked at least ten blocks away and then you walked the one you had caught back to the bus. Now that was the absolute highlight of the event. And we did do that. And if he was interested, he'd come back the next week. And it was all very fun. It was all very fun at that time."

Gradually, however, by her last years in high school, the matter shifted from blending in with to standing out from the others. "I always liked to have some award or something."

Deciding how this could be accomplished was confused by the fact that she received conflicting signals from her teachers—some singling her out for her abilities, others shunning her for her excessive blackness. Not given to introspection, Barbara began to study the situation in order to create a niche for herself. And what that was took awhile to establish.

I don't know when I became aware of any ability of mine. At first I did not use this in any good way, but just to outsmart my teachers, which I did with some regularity. I remember a science teacher who just laid me out one day before the rest of the kids. I recall I had read this particular science lesson the preceding day, although I wasn't much of a serious student, but I did want to have a general idea of what was going to occur in class. And this teacher was up explaining something and I held up my hand and said: "That's not right. It is this way." And she laid me out. She said: "You think you're so smart." And she went and reported my smart-aleckness to Aunt Mamie.

Also, other teachers reported that I would talk to my friends in class, during the class, and apparently would do this at a volume that was disruptive. So they told Aunt

Mamie, and Mamie—she never was heavyhanded—she would just say to me: "Well, you ought not to do that, because I don't want to tell Ben about your behavior." So that settled it. And after a while I got it under control.

Besides, I knew that at some point I would go to college, because Rose Mary was already at Prairie View and it was sort of understood in my family that you would go to college. Now, I had visited Prairie View and I didn't want that view of the prairie. I preferred to stay right in Houston, where I would have free run of the city, but I knew I would go to college.

So I started to think maybe I should take school more seriously. It also pleased me when I had discovered I was brighter than a lot of the kids in my class. And I spent some time tutoring some of my fellow classmates. I would go through geometry problems with them, or try to familiarize them with chemistry lingo. It makes it a more rewarding experience to go to school if you feel, as in my instance, that you're a little brighter than your classmates.

Now I was also learning that the world had decided that we were all Negro, but that some of us were more Negro than others. The whole system at that time was saying to us that you achieved more, you went further, you had a better chance, you got the awards, if you were not black-black with kinky hair. Black was bad and you didn't want to be black, and so the message we were getting was that you were really in tough shape and it was too bad that you were so unfortunate that your skin was totally black and there was no light there anywhere. Some of the kids started using bleaching cream. Black and White Bleaching Cream. It would have been desirable to pass for white if you could have, but few had enough features of a white person to do that.

That whole thing reminded me of the occasion in elementary school of my appearance in a play. It was, I suppose, my first public presentation. What really struck me about it was that I played the role of a maid, and my mother went on a bus to J. C. Penney to buy my outfit for this play, a blue maid's uniform with little white cuffs on it. And I thought: Why would this little elementary school, all black, have presented a play with a maid? That struck me as ironic.

I did not think it right for blacks to be in one place and whites in another place and never shall the two meet. There was just something about that that didn't feel right to me. And I wanted that to change, but I also had those feelings that it was going to be this way for a long, long time, and that nobody was going to be able to do anything to change it. It was a fatalistic kind of acceptance of what was, and we had that at that time.

I felt nobody could change it because it just seemed so big that it was everywhere. I had no quarter of experience which I could relate to to say: "But it's different there." So it was massive and I felt that no one would be able to change it because it was something bigger than anyone I knew. And it wasn't only the school system, it was everywhere. The church, the city. We would ride on the back of the bus and there was a sign on the bus with a little colored bar, and you had to walk back there to sit.

We would go to Weingarten's to shop, and there were drinking fountains, one of which said *White* and one said *Colored;* and you couldn't go to the bathroom because most of the time there was none for blacks, and if there was, it was separated from the main rooms for men and women, in the back of the building with an outside entrance. We would go downtown and there were people sitting and eating and enjoying themselves—and it was all a totally white world. There was nothing you saw to indicate that a black person and a white person could be together on a friendly basis. You saw the porters and the maids, but to see a black person in some other capacity, in a white shirt with a tie, was nonexistent. The idea of a black going to a hotel for any purpose other than for a back-door delivery was impossible. And looking at how widespread this was, my feeling was, well, this is just it. I guess it's always going to be this way.

As a student at Phillis Wheatley High School, seeing all of that, I decided that if I was going to be outstanding or different, it was going to have to be in relation to other black people rather than in some setting where white people were.

Somewhere in this time, when everybody but about five of us were saying they were going to be teachers, I began to announce that I was going to be a lawyer. I believed I was going to be a lawyer, or rather something called a lawyer, but I had no fixed notion of what that was. Charles White at that time was going to be a doctor. Otis King said he was going to be a lawyer, and later he was. Samuel Biggers said he was going to be a doctor, and he became one. Joan Martin went to the School of Social Work in Atlanta. Charles White did not become a doctor, but I don't know what happened—whether he tried to make it and couldn't, or not. But the point was, we were too sheltered to know that we didn't know what we were talking about in these aspirations; we didn't know what was entailed. What I'm saying is, at the time when I decided that I was not going to be like the rest, my point of reference was other black people. It seemed an impossibility to make any transition to that larger world out there.

What I regret is that some of the teachers fed into that whole attitude that if you were whiter you got a better chance, instead of saying: "Look, this is the way it is, but it doesn't have to be that way."

There was one teacher I didn't like too well, because I felt that she was color-struck—that's what we called it. I felt that she favored all the people who had fair skin and good hair. Teachers of her bias favored those who had hair that wasn't nappy, hair that didn't require Excellento, straighter hair. That's what it was: a better grade of hair. This was a really big factor that all of us could see clearly, and one reason that I could always detect when favoritism was being shown by the teacher to the half-white kids was that they became the attendants of Miss Wheatley, the student elected as the symbol of the high school.

Well, at this time Evelyn Cunningham, the dean of girls, approached me to run for tenth-grade attendant to Miss Wheatley. Now I felt I would be totally out of place, that I would feel too uncomfortable to present myself for that part. I had accepted the judgment of the times and decided that I wasn't going to change any attitudes. So I said: "Miss Cunningham, I am not the right light color, and I don't have the clothes, the whole thing." And she says: "Well, I really think you could do that, because you are a popular student, with lots of friends around." But I did not want to attend Miss Wheatley.

My geometry teacher, Exa O'Daye Hardin, was my favorite. I liked her and she liked me. She was one of those saying to me that I didn't have enough confidence in myself, and she gave me a good deal of tough talk about confidence and she'd tell me about what kind of head I had, that sort of thing. So she figured, if I was not going to attend, I should try something else. And I thought about it, and I thought: What I can be is Girl of the Year.

She was chosen by a national black sorority that looked over a roster of senior girls to select the one who was most outstanding. And I thought: Girl of the Year is a better thing to be than an attendant, because all of the clubs and organizations give you a gift. And you are not attending anyone else. So I had in the back of my mind, long before anyone thought of it, that that's what I would be. But I didn't tell this to anybody at the time.

Teachers used to require you to memorize certain passages of things, and you stood up and recited them. Now, I had done that all my life. At Greater Pleasant Hill I had done that. I knew I always enjoyed doing that. So at Wheatley I began to speak, and it became apparent to others that I could do public speaking. With this kind of awareness on the part of the teachers, the sponsor of the declamation oratorical contest, Mr. Ashton Jerome Olivier, asked me to participate. Which I did.

He would take us in his beige Pontiac to Prairie View College, where the black state meets were always held, and of course you went through local and regional and district levels before you ever got to that point, but I did on many occasions get to that point, and I would be the winner and bring home the medals. Then we would have a ceremony and a presentation of the trophies to the school. And we declaimers and debaters felt self-important with the little box of three-by-five-inch index cards on which we kept our notes. These were our badge of superiority over the others who could not do things like that.

And I was also working with those school clubs which were well-respected by other students, because I was still working toward being Girl of the Year. I was a member of the Wheatley Lovable Troubadors. Now I don't recall who the Troubadors were, but it was a very well-respected club among the kids. And the teacher who was the sponsor was a very influential person on the faculty, and she was one of the ones who was color-struck, so I wanted to make a good impression on her.

And then the honor society; I believe I was president of that. And I had made friendships with the brightest kids who might be my competitors. These people were my friends, my genuine friends, including Mary Elizabeth Justice and Joan Martin, and in trying to weigh my qualifications for Girl of the Year against theirs, I decided that the thing I had which they didn't was going and doing all that declaiming, oratory, getting all the medals and trophies. I thought: That ought to give me one-uppance on anybody else.

And of course it did. The word came in my senior year: "We have selected Barbara Jordan Girl of the Year."

I got home and was telling my folks about it, my mother and father, when I saw we had a problem. I told them: "You know there's a special program for the presentation of this Girl of the Year, and I don't have anything to wear for a special occasion like this. The best-looking thing I have is the beige suit with the light-blue blouse, but I have just worn that out and I don't have anything else." My mother said: "I guess that is a problem." Then the geometry teacher, Exa Hardin, called my mother and said she would help dress me for the presentation. And my mother thanked her and said we would let her know. Then Mamie called us, having received the news, and said to my mother: "Arlyne, the thing for me to do is to go to Sakowitz and buy Barbara a dress for the presentation, and I'll charge it on my account, and you can pay me back any way you want to." My mother said: "Now that sounds like an acceptable solution to this." And it was an off-white lace dress from Sakowitz that cost thirty-five dollars, and I thought it was just beautiful. And my mother paid Mamie back five dollars a week at church until Mamie said she would handle the rest of it. And I was Girl of the Year in 1952.

There was a table where the clubs put their gifts—pen sets, and books, and boxes of stationery, and handkerchiefs —high school graduation-type gifts, and my mother and father came, and my acceptance speech was really super. I can't pull it out of my head any more, but I had people in tears. It was so moving that my father couldn't stand it. I know it began: "This is the happiest moment of my life."

But the big thing was the Ushers contest. My debate coach suggested that I participate in the Ushers Oratorical Contest. So I went to Waco with a group of solid black Baptists and participated in the state contest and won first prize—my first prize at Waco being fifty dollars and an all-expense-paid trip to Chicago to participate in the National Ushers Convention Oratorical Contest. My mother said: "Well, we'll go to Chicago."

Now I had done the same thing with the Elks contest, won first prize in the state and then gone on to the finals and been the runner-up. One thing I had learned from that experience was that I didn't like losing. But one of the judges in the Elks contest, Tom Freeman, who later became my debate coach at Texas Southern University, told me after the thousand-dollar Elks award was presented to the winner, that he thought I should have won and that he gave me first place on his card. Now I didn't know what I did wrong to lose Elks, but I did see that the winners of those contests, who were all male, were very skilled in histrionics and always very dramatic in their presentations. So I made a note of that, and we headed for Chicago.

The swing, the unsteadiness of the train, was a big surprise to me. It was a new thing. And after I looked at all the people in the car with their box lunches, which they had bought somewhere, and compared them with ours, which we had brought from home in brown bags, I struck up a conversation with the conductor. And he said: "There's a vacant chair car down the way and I've got some time." So I left Mother and went with him and he regaled me with tales of his travels up and down the railroad line and how many women he had in all the towns along the way. And I thought: "This must be the life, seeing different people and going different places. The train must be the way to go."

We were met at the Chicago train station by some of the Ushers who had been at Waco, and who knew us from there, and taken to the Greater Bethesda Baptist Church where the contest was to be held.

When the big night came, I wore my pink evening dress from the All Girls' Choir Recital and sat with the other contestants in the church choir loft where we drew for order of speakers. When our time came, we each left our seat and went down from the loft to stand on the platform and give our speech into the microphone before the audience and the judges. We had memorized our speeches already as they were the same ones we had given in the state contests. So mine was the speech I gave in Waco. The subject was: "Is the Necessity for a Higher Education More in Demand Today than a Decade Ago?"

While I sat there listening to the others, I of course compared myself to them, deciding that I would knock that one off, or I would really top that one. So by the time I got down there to the microphone I felt that I was going to wow them. I don't know how it could have been possible, but I really felt that they had never heard the word before about higher education that I was going to give them, and that it was probably going to be the great revelation of their lives.

When my turn came, I let them have it:

"Today we are living in a world of chaos and upheaval. Each day the world is changing.

"Each day men and women are entering new fields of endeavor, and the necessity for a higher education to meet the needs of the people is more and more in demand.

"The necessity for a higher education is more in demand today than a decade ago, first because of the increasing attempts on the part of our foreign neighbors to do away with our democracy.

"A higher education is more necessary today than it was ten years ago because of the increasing effect American education has on our culture.

"We need a higher education today in dealing with our present social problems.

"Finally, the necessity for a higher education is more in demand today than a decade ago because today's youth are living in a confused world. You are not only refusing to one out of two of the youth in this country the opportunity to do the work for which they have been preparing themselves, but you are also deliberately refusing to give them the intellectual and moral guidance they need and that the world of tomorrow is to need."

It went something like that. But the main thing I was saying was: "Folks, a higher education is on the way in. It's the only way out." I was saying: "It's the only way out of the fix you're in."

I felt very good about the way I delivered the speech, and when I finished, I knew that I had given it just the way I wanted to give it. So I thought when I sat down: If I don't take first place on this one, I never will. But I did, and that was fine. I was riding on a great big high.

░

Barbara gave the Houston *Informer* (July 27, 1952), the black newspaper that wanted to interpolate some greater victory from her speech, the statement expected of her: one line of fitting rhetoric to run beneath her featured photograph, and a lengthy list of her laudable accomplishments:

"Miss Barbara Charline Jordan, daughter of the Reverend and Mrs. B. M. Jordan of 4910 Campbell, added to her long list of oratorical awards the state award of the United Ushers Association, held July 3 in Waco. Miss Jordan competed with contestants from all over the state of Texas. For winning first place she received $50 and an all-expense-paid trip to the National United Ushers Association of America in Chicago, held in the Greater Bethesda Baptist Church, July 21 through 25.

"In the national convention contest held Thursday night, July 24, at 8:00 P.M., Miss Jordan represented the state of Texas and competed with contestants from nine other states, including New York, Massachusetts, Illinois, Ohio, and others. She won first place and received a $200 scholarship to the school of her choice and a literary medal. Miss Jordan chose as her subject: Is the Necessity for a Higher Education More in Demand Today than a Decade Ago?

"A spring honor graduate from the Phillis Wheatley

high school, the talented young woman won the praise and congratulations from educational circles all over the state. She held the distinction of having been chosen 'Girl of the Year' by the Zeta Phi Beta sorority, and is winner of the Julius Levy Oratorical Contest award, a gold medal centered with a diamond. She also holds three district and two state championship medals in Junior and Senior declamation, respectively, and a medal for outstanding accomplishments in speech.

"Very modest and reserved, Miss Jordan had a short but forceful statement to give to the *Informer* in a well-modulated voice about this latest accomplishment: 'It's just another milestone I have passed; it's just the beginning.'"

Closer to her real feelings about the trip to Illinois, spent in a black cocoon as tight as Good Hope on Sunday morning, was the gushing comment in her yearbook, typical of any high school graduate:

"My trip to Chicago was the most Wonderful, Enjoyable, Exciting, Adventurous, Adorable, Unforgettable, Rapturous—it was just the best doggone trip I have ever had."

It had been great to ride those big metal wheels, and fine to win the Ushers prize. But Barbara had not yet left home.

TWO

WHITE WORLD

"I realized, starkly, that the best training available in an all-black, instant university was not equal. Separate was not equal, no matter what face you put on it. It came to me that you couldn't just say something was so, because somebody brighter, smarter, more thoughtful would come out and tell you it wasn't so. Then if you still thought it was, you had to prove it. I really can't describe what that did to my insides and to my head. I said I'm being educated, finally. I'm doing sixteen years of remedial work in thinking."

4. BOSTON

At first, Texas Southern University seemed an extension of Phillis Wheatley High School: a continuation of the black strip of Houston, of riding around in cars with Bennie and the crowd, of feuding with her father.

First order of business, the matter of getting enrolled. Figuring out how most pleasantly to pass the interim three years until she could get into TSU's law school and become the lawyer she had vaguely claimed she wanted to be, Barbara arrived at the administration building and went up to a course adviser at a table marked PRE-LAW. When she asked what she should take, they said: "Nothing special. Whatever you want. Just credits." So she looked over the list of courses open to freshmen and signed up for some philosophy, some psychology, some English, math, and science. Thinking: "Fine, I'll play around three years."

Next order of business, concerning settling down to have a good time, was sorority. Bennie belonged to the Delta Sigma Thetas, and Barbara thought if what you did, with the Justices off at other schools, was join a Greek organization, fine, that's what she would do. When they all went to drink beer at the Groovy Grill, she wanted to be there, socializing, too. This meant getting a job baby-sitting and house-cleaning—as Ben had refused to pay anything toward a "hellfire sorority"—so that she could pay her dues. At the first rush party, held on the campus at dusk in front of the old administration building so that everyone could see you having a good time, Barbara watched the Big Sisters put on a costumed skit for the prospective pledges and thought that she would like to do that, get up there and sing her specialty, "Money, Honey," and wear the Delta colors, red and white, and sing their song, "How would you like to be a Delta girl, umph and a little bit more . . ." So she was happy to join the club.

Then followed a lot of driving around and drinking which got her into trouble at home. One night a lady from the Greater Pleasant Hill Baptist Church caught Barbara and Bennie drinking beer in the Grill, and reported back to the pastor, Ben Jordan, that his girls had been seen in a public place at a table littered with "red caps."

When Bennie got home, Ben raged at her, reducing her to near tears as, trembling and defensive, she tried to explain her way out of it. When Barbara arrived home to find this scene she asked, "What's the problem here?" "I'll tell you what the problem is," her father snapped. "I have been informed that all you and your sister do at Texas Southern University is sit around and drink beer."

"Well, if somebody said that's all we do, they lied. They lied," she stated, going into her room and slamming the door, putting an end to the matter, knowing that there was nothing further he could do about it.

She was used to operating on her own, doing what she wanted to do. The first week of school, after registration,

Barbara, looking around to continue her list of honors, filed for student body president, thinking that would be a nice place to start, but when the dean of women informed her that freshmen were definitely not eligible for that office, she decided to stick to what was familiar: the prestigious three-by-five cards.

The debate coach turned out to be the one judge in the Elks Oratorical Contest who had given her first place —ebullient, bustling Tom Freeman. So that was a fine coincidence. For his part, he was delighted to take her on and bring her up to his standards. "She was good at projecting herself," he commented, "but she was not good at thinking. I put her on constructive affirmative, which was presentation, letting the boys do the refutation until she got the hang of it."

Tom Freeman, who had attended Virginia Union University and Andover Newton Seminary, taken courses at Boston University and Harvard, and received his doctorate in homiletics (preaching) at the University of Chicago, picked up where Mamie Lee left off—zealously expanding the options that were offered his kids from an all-black world.

"I'd take students around the country in order to let them practice the normal skills and competencies against such schools as Chicago and Boston. I wanted them to hold their own. I wanted them to learn to think.

"I did it by tossing out ideas and letting them argue back. I was single then and they'd all come to my house. I had a kind of pal relationship which involved intimacy and interaction. I gave them a sense that they could handle themselves anywhere, as most of them had been robbed of the sense of worth due to the oppression put upon them."

He wrote friends at schools in the East and told them

that the Texas Southern University debate team was on tour, and would they get an audience together and set up a schedule. Then, piling them into his annual new car, he let his boys take on the best opposition they could find. He considered that they won every debate: the fact of their being there was winning.

Barbara, entranced at the thought of driving around the country with Tom and his debaters in a fancy yellow Mercury, did what she could to make him break his policy of never taking females along. She gave up the scoop-neck dresses and costume jewelry of high school, cropped her waved hair short above her ears, affected bulky, boxy jackets and flat shoes. Gaining twenty pounds, her buxom figure took on the squared lines of androgyny. She became a no-nonsense presence, someone it was all right to take across the country in a car full of males and not worry about chaperonage.

These were very different trips from her excursion to Chicago for the Ushers; this time she was plunged into the middle of the outside world's racial discrimination. Tom and his "ragtag debaters" would pack the car with boxes of fruit and sandwiches and fried chicken, so as not to be dependent on locating black cafés in the states bordering Texas. They had a map circled with black motels. If this was Barbara's first exposure to travel in a white world, it was an old, bitter experience for Tom. It ate at him constantly that his kids could not use the restaurants or bathrooms along the way. He carried on a continuous argument with service-station attendants because they offered only restrooms for Men, Women, and Colored, the latter being outhouses in a field. One evening, when the food boxes were empty and his ire was up at the sight of his tired, hungry crew, he resolved: "I'm going to see if we can get something to eat here." He stormed into a barbeque place to try to buy food for his debaters. Told that if he brought them around to the back door of the kitchen they could eat there, he dug in his heels and took what he could get for them.

But arrival at Chicago, Boston, New York, Cambridge, was vindication. "We didn't eat at any fancy restaurants," he said. "We didn't have that kind of money to spend. But we could at least go in front doors to get something to eat. That was the main point: we could go in the front door."

Back at home, doors began to open also. In 1954, Barbara's junior year in college, the Supreme Court faced up to the language and the facts it had avoided so long, declaring in unequivocal terms that "separate" could never be "equal." In *Brown* v. *The Board of Education*, a civil rights agitator had brought to trial a case involving black schoolchildren segregated in ostensibly equal facilities. The question raised was: "Does segregation of children in public schools solely on the basis of race, even though the physical facilities and other 'tangible' factors may be equal, deprive the children of the minority group of equal educational opportunities?" The answer: "We believe that it does."

Going back to where they had left off with Sweatt, the Court reiterated: ". . . in deciding that a segregated law school could not provide equal educational opportunities, this Court relied in large part on 'those qualities which are incapable of objective measurement . . .'" Extending that, they stated: "Such considerations apply with added force to children in grade and high schools. To separate them from others of similar age and qualifications solely because of their race generates a feeling of inferiority as to their status in the community that may affect their hearts and

minds in a way unlikely ever to be undone." Citing the
Kansas lower court, they quoted: " 'Segregation of white
and colored children in public schools has a detrimental
effect upon the colored children. The impact is greater
when it has the sanction of the law; for the policy of sepa-
rating the races is usually interpreted as denoting the inferiority of the Negro group. A sense of inferiority affects
the motivation of a child to learn. Segregation with the
sanction of law, therefore, has a tendency to [retard] the
educational and mental development of Negro children and
to deprive them of some of the benefits they would receive
in a racial[ly] integrated school system.' Whatever may
have been the extent of psychological knowledge at the
time of *Plessy* v. *Ferguson*, this [present] finding is amply
supported by modern authority. Any language in *Plessy* v.
Ferguson contrary to this finding is rejected.

"We conclude that in the field of public education the
doctrine of 'separate but equal' has no place. Separate
educational facilities are inherently unequal."

Barbara was elated at the decision. "So finally," she
said, "those kids in elementary and high schools are going
to be able to go to school with white kids, and that's going
to be good. I wish it had happened a few years earlier so
I could have been with those white kids myself, because
I would have loved it. But they sure have something to
look forward to."

Reading banner headlines in the *Informer* with jubilant
quotes from the NAACP, she supposed integration would
be immediate, assumed that the students at such places as
Phillis Wheatley would be the beneficiaries of that racial
mix in a week or so. "But all due speed was no speed at all.
As far as Houston, Texas, was concerned, the Supreme
Court had not said a word."

The long-desired decision and the silence following it gnawed at her. She carried it in the back of her mind when Baylor University in Waco opened its doors to the Southern Forensic Conference. Tom Freeman, who had entered her in the contest at once, drove her up the road so that she could match herself against whites on a one-to-one basis. It felt good, she told him, to have this chance to test her oratory against these different people. As he watched from the back of the classroom she launched into a recitation: "We are poor little lambs who have lost our way. We are little black sheep who have gone astray. Lord, have mercy on such as we . . ."

When she won first prize, as she had done so often before, she thought: "Why, you white girls are no competition at all. If this is the best you have to offer, I haven't missed anything."

But winning did not feel the same. She had won at Waco already, at the Ushers contest. It was going to take more than one more medal to do anything for the children who still had to play the black maid in elementary-school presentations. She thought back to her high school days, to the pompous, vague debates championing integration when she had felt that it could never come to pass because the problem was so big no one could move it. But now the courts had done that; they had moved it. And still nothing was happening. "I woke to the necessity that someone had to push integration along in a private way if it were ever going to come. That was on my mind continually at that period—that some black people could make it in this white man's world, and that those who could had to do it. They had to move."

Reviewing her own future, she came to a decision. "Look," she told herself, "I don't know whether law school is going to work out for you; you've got all these courses and they don't equip you to do anything but stay at TSU." So she got her transcript and pieced together what she could get if she stayed a fourth year, settling on a bachelor's degree in government, settling on a program which would let her get out of the state to law school.

When a Harvard debate team came to TSU to debate Tom's stars, and Barbara and Otis King tied them, she announced: "I want to go to Harvard Law School. I want to go to the best, and Harvard is the best."

"You can't get in Harvard," Tom told her. "They have never heard of Texas Southern University at Harvard Law School. My brother was an honor graduate of Virginia Union, and he couldn't get in; but he went to Boston University, and then he got in Harvard for postgraduate work. Boston is just across the river."

So Barbara, who wanted to go where she was wanted, took his advice. "Well," she said, "I'll write to Boston."

Which she did, not breathing a word to anyone at home about what she had in mind. Then, after the catalogues came and she studied the cost of tuition and books and room and board, she finally carried them into the living room one evening and laid it on her father. "This is where I want to go to law school."

Never able to put herself back in time to her father's early manhood, never able to understand the frustrated ambition in this man who was always instigating some venture, trying to get ahead, longing for prominence, Barbara, this black sheep of the family, had no concept of what it had meant to him to get into Tuskegee—and then to have to leave. She dismissed his days there when anyone asked, with: "Oh, well, my father always said he studied black-smithing, but why would anyone do that when you knew that the horse would not always be the mode of transportation used by everyone?"

Studying the financial facts about Boston University, hoping again one more time that this unlikely daughter might improbably be the one to do what he had not been able to do himself, Ben offered all he had: "This is more money than I have ever spent on anything or anyone. But if you want to go, we'll manage. But if I pay for you to go up there, there won't be any money for you to come home for Thanksgiving, Christmas, Easter. Once you get there, you're there."

But this was always true of Barbara: Wherever she was, she was there. Although this time *there* turned out to be a harder world than she could have conceived.

Going to Boston was my first departure from the womb. I'd been living at home, being the chief of my own tiny little world, and here I was going farther away than anybody in my family had ever been.

Tom Freeman had inspired more people than myself to seek graduate training in Boston. One other was George Turner, from Wharton, Texas, who was on the debating team while I was on the debating team. He was going to Andover Newton Theological Seminary because Tom Freeman had gone there for his divinity degree. So George said to me: "Since we're both going to Boston, why don't we drive up there together in my car?" In the meantime, Issie Shelton, who had been Girl of the Year at Jack Yates High School when I was Girl of the Year at Phillis Wheatley, was also going to Boston University Law

School. She knew I was going to Boston, as this was well-publicized in the *Informer*, and so she called, and we decided to all go in a group.

George said he was going to buy a car, and he did, an old slant-back beige Buick. Our trunks had been shipped by railway express, but we had to load the car with all the necessities, because George anticipated that it was going to take us about three days, and we needed clothing to wear for the time we were up there before school actually started and a lot of food so that we could ride for a day without stopping to eat in any place of public accommodation. George said it was a sound car, that its only problem was it leaked oil. So he had purchased a case of oil that had to go in the back seat, where I was riding, so he could put oil in whenever we stopped at a filling station. Issie was in the front seat with George, and I was in the back seat, which was half filled with luggage and boxes and things for school—and the case of oil, which was on the floor. I had only a tiny corner in which to sit for this ride, and I was not tiny at that time.

George had mapped out our trip; he had designated the places we could stay through the South. So we proceeded. And every time we stopped, the service-station attendant would fill the car with gas and he would say: "You are low on oil." Then George would jump out and say: "I got my own oil." Then he would add a quart or two and away we'd go. At night we got two rooms—rooms at that time were a small cost—one for George and one for Issie and me. He would wake up and decide if we had time for breakfast, as he had worked out the schedule. All we had to do was ride.

Eventually we got there. Issie was not staying in university housing; she had arranged for an apartment. George took her there. I had a letter that said I would be staying at 2 Rawley Street. But when I got out of the car and went in, I found a note taped to the table that said: "This dormitory is not yet ready for occupancy. All residents of Rawley Street should go to Charlesgate East." So George drove until we found that place and I unloaded my bags at Charlesgate and got a room and bid him goodbye. And bedded down for the evening.

The first night in that room I was asking: "What in the world, Barbara Jordan, are you doing here?" I said: "Now, if you were at home right now you would be much happier, you'd get in Dad's car, and get Bennie, and pick up the Justices, and you'd probably go and buy some barbeque and a couple of beers, and here you are in this strange place."

All right, so in three days I moved to 2 Rawley Street. The university had sent me a form on which I had to indicate whether I wanted a black roommate or a white roommate, or whether it didn't matter. I had checked it did not matter, because it didn't. So I went to my room and I had a black roommate, LaConyea Butler, who was working on a master's degree.

There was a young woman there at the desk who said: "Someone has been looking for you." I said: "For me?" And she said: "Yes, a person who is going to enroll at B. U. Law School heard that there was to be one other person in this graduate dorm enrolling in B. U. Law School, and she really wants to meet you." And I said: "Well, then."

So I met Louise. Louise was my good friend that freshman year. Her father was John Bailey, who was chairman of the Democratic National Committee at that time. Louise was what I always viewed as the typical rich white girl. That was Louise. And to encounter her so early as a friend

—well, I said, that's why I wanted to come here, to meet these people. Louise's father, in addition to being chairman of the Democratic National Committee, was also a well-positioned lawyer in Hartford, Connecticut, and a graduate of Harvard Law School. And Louise's father had given her for college graduation a new black Ford convertible that had that Lincoln Continental look with the raised tire on the back. Well, I was almost out of my skull. Look what I'd run into the first day. Right there.

So, after overcoming the initial strangeness of being in Boston and being closed off over there at Charlesgate East those first few nights, I settled in. Louise had a room in the attic, which was converted to rooms, and I had a roommate, because I preferred not to be in the room by myself. My funds were pretty tight at that point and I hadn't counted on the forty-cents-a-day subway ride to law school, hadn't counted on it not being right there. Didn't know it was up a steep hill. So I had to factor in the subway out of my spending money. My father had taken care of tuition and room and board, and that was a significant amount of money. A very significant amount. And Rose Mary had paid for my books. In terms of the cash I had available, it was twenty dollars a month: ten from Rose Mary and ten from Bennie, who had decided they would take care of my spending money out of their school-teaching salaries. I figured I could make it on that: forty cents a day for subway, and food was paid for, and I would have a little left over for a movie.

I wasn't going to work, didn't think I should work, as I figured the law was going to be enough for me to contend with. And so I could make it on what Rose Mary and Bennie sent me.

One weekend Louise wanted to go home and she had run out of cash, and she came and said: "Could you lend

me some money?" And I said: "Sure." Naturally I wasn't
going to say that I couldn't afford it. I said: "Sure, how
much do you want?" And she said: "Five dollars." To get
the train to Hartford or something, to flip-flop to Hartford
for the weekend. So I got my billfold, patting the contents
to try to see if it was going to figure, and all I had was one
of my ten-dollar bills. And of course, I said: "Why don't
you just take the ten?" A real sport. I don't know what I
would have done if she hadn't paid me back. I just had to
lend her the money.

She said she'd leave me the new black Ford while she
was gone, but I didn't feel I should drive her car. I didn't
feel I was supposed to do that, as it had turned out we did
not go anywhere in Louise's car, didn't ride around the
way I was used to. And that was a disappointment.

So I went to the law school and walked into a room with
all freshman law school students, about six hundred, because that was in the days when the attrition rate was aw-
fully high—they'd get in all that money from freshmen,
and then half of them would punch out. There were six
women, and Issie and I were the two black women. And
we were all assembled there and they were giving the orientation and telling us about the classrooms, and where
they were located, and about the *Law Review*, and I was
back there saying: "I'll make the *Law Review*. I'll take
care of that."

Now, Issie, my friend Issie, who had gone to Indiana
University, knew a little more about what she was getting
into than I did, and so when I said that, she just kind of
laughed. But I didn't know how funny that was until we
started the courses of study.

Everything was so different to me. *Contracts, property,
torts* were strange words to me. Words I had not dealt

with. And there I was. It appeared that everybody else's
father was a lawyer. Everybody's father was a lawyer, and
they talked about working in their father's law office in the
summer, and what they did there, how they helped him to
breathe. Can you understand how strange this was to my
ears? This was a language that I had not heard before.
How could I hear it? From anybody? To them it was so
familiar, it was just like mother's milk.

And the contracts professor, he started marching up and
down talking about *promisor* and *promisee*. And I said:
"For crying out loud." And then he said: "For all of you
who have girlfriends or boyfriends, say good day to them
when you return home this evening, because you won't see
them any more this year. But don't tell them you will see
them later, no, tell them you will see them subsequently."
He said: "You have to learn to talk that way."

The only thing that sounded familiar to me was criminal
law—because you could read in the newspaper about
murder and rape, and they didn't talk about *lessor* and *les-
see* and *promisor* and *promisee*. I could understand a bur-
glary.

Now the classes began and there was no review of subject matter at all. You would be taught for the entire year
and there would be one examination, at the end of the
year. I couldn't get ready for that. I said: "Looks like they
ought to give us little periodic quizzes, to see whether
we're understanding it at all."

The only exam I had at midterm was criminal law, because it was a half-year course. And I thought: "This is my
familiar subject, because I understand the words. So this is
my absolute first test. And I think I've got it, think I'm
ready for it."

But the questions were, as I recall, phrased in what I felt

was an ambiguous way, so that several answers would suffice, and I saw that that was the way it was supposed to be. It was apparent to me that in the questions what was being tested was not so much your answer but how you reached the answer you gave. That was the point of the exam: If you could say how you got wherever you got, if that was clear, you did all right. I was unaccustomed to a question being presented to me in an examination where I would have to talk about various approaches and decide how this approach was the more logical of the alternatives. So that's what I had trouble with, because the questions were not phrased so you could say: "Yes, he's guilty," or: "No, he's not guilty." You had to think it through, and that was something I had not developed. I suppose those people that worked in those law offices all the summers, in their dads' offices, they could do that. What I couldn't focus on during the exam was that it was not the answer that the professor was trying to pull from me, it was the reasoning.

So I decided right then and there that I had punched out totally. I took whatever money I had and went to a movie. I couldn't talk. I didn't want anybody to talk to me, and I thought: The safest thing to do is to go into a movie and sit down in the dark. And I sat there for three hours wondering how I was going to lay it on my father that I had just busted out of law school.

Well, I didn't flunk the exam; I made a 79, but I didn't know this until the grades came out several weeks later. Meanwhile I had not gone home for Christmas. They kept a dormitory open for the foreign students and those who couldn't go home. So I packed up with the Koreans and the Greeks and went to whichever dorm was being kept open for those of us who couldn't go home.

Now, the logical question would be: If Louise was my

very good friend, why didn't she invite me to go to Hartford, which I could have afforded to do? But I didn't expect that I was going to be tottling off to their big house. I knew I was not to do that.

So Louise called on Christmas to wish me a Merry Christmas, and I thanked her for inquiring about my well-being.

I had learned that you see what works and you see what gets turned down. It's a sense of how you are received. You drop by a room, or you walk into a study group, or you suggest that you have a cup of coffee together—and that is either accepted or rejected. So it's just trial and error. I learned that white people love to stop doing whatever they're doing and go have a cup of coffee. That was always a sure one. You knew you could do that. So I did that in the dorm. Went by and invited people to stop by and have a cup of coffee. And in the big world out there it might sound trite, but people discussed issues and ideas of substance in general conversation. They were very well read; they could discuss books, and, of course, a lot of our conversation focused on law school and legal issues and points of law, and we would get into discussions about that. I learned to do that. I started to talk about going to the Boston Pops and all that, because you couldn't be narrowly focused, you had to have a broad range of things that you could talk about, that were interesting. And if I could pinpoint anything, it was that the most important lesson was that you always had to be prepared. You were a dodo if you were not prepared. You always had to be a day early. Early so that when the day came, you sort of had it well in hand. Whatever you were talking about, class or your private discussion, you had to be prepared. I knew I could not catch up. It would take a lifetime. I'd have to be born again and just come from another mother's womb and have a totally different kind of upbringing. My whole life would have to be different. It was not a matter of trying to catch up. You couldn't. What you wanted to do was slot in right where you were and deal with that, and you knew that you had to work extraordinarily hard to function right there, where you were.

So I was at Boston University in this new and strange and different world, and it occurred to me that if I was going to succeed at this strange new adventure, I would have to read longer and more thoroughly than my colleagues at law school had to read. I felt that in order to compensate for what I had missed in earlier years, I would have to work harder, and study longer, than anybody else. I still had this feeling that I did not want my colleagues to know what a tough time I was having understanding the concepts, the words, the ideas, the process. I didn't want them to know that. So I did my reading not in the law library, but in a library at the graduate dorm, upstairs where it was very quiet, because apparently nobody else there studied. So I would go there at night after dinner. I would load my books under my arm and go to the library, and I would read until the wee hours of the morning and then go to bed. I didn't get much sleep during those years. I was lucky if I got three or four hours a night, because I had to stay up. I had to. The professors would assign cases for the next day, and these cases had to be read and understood or I would be behind, further behind than I was.

I was always delighted when I would get called upon to recite in class. But the professors did not call on the "ladies" very much. There were certain favored people who always got called on, and then on some rare occasions a professor would come in and would announce: "We're going to have Ladies Day today." And he would call on the ladies. We were just tolerated. We weren't considered really top drawer when it came to the study of the law.

At some time in the spring, Bill Gibson, who was dating my new roomate, Norma Walker, organized a black study group, as we blacks had to form our own. This was because we were not invited into any of the other study groups. There were six or seven in our group—Bill, and Issie, and I think Maynard Jackson—and we would just gather and talk it out and hear ourselves do that. One thing I learned was that you had to talk out the issues, the facts, the cases, the decisions, the process. You couldn't just read the cases and study alone in your library as I had been doing; and you couldn't get it all in the classroom. But once you had talked it out in the study group, it flowed more easily and made a lot more sense.

And from time to time I would go up to the fourth floor at 2 Rawley Street to check on how Louise was doing. She was always reading *Redbook*. Every time I was in there and wanted to discuss one of the cases with her, she was reading a short story in *Redbook*. I don't know how she could do that. She was not prepared in class when the professors would call on her to discuss cases, but that did not bother her. Whereas it was a matter of life and death with me. I had to make law school. I just didn't have any alternatives. I could not afford to flunk out. That would have been an unmitigated disaster. So I read all the time I was not in class.

Finally I felt I was really learning things, really going to school. I felt that I was getting educated, whatever that was. I became familiar with the process of thinking. I learned to think things out and reach conclusions and defend what I had said.

In the past I had got along by spouting off. Whether you talked about debates or oratory, you dealt with speechifying. Even in debate it was pretty much canned because you had, in your little three-by-five box, a response for whatever issue might be raised by the opposition. The format was structured so that there was no opportunity for independent thinking. (I really had not had my ideas challenged ever.) But I could no longer orate and let that pass for reasoning. Because there was not any demand for an orator in Boston University Law School. You had to think and read and understand and reason. I had learned at twenty-one that you couldn't just say a thing is so because it might not be so, and somebody brighter, smarter, and more thoughtful would come out and tell you it wasn't so. Then, if you still thought it was, you had to prove it. Well, that was a new thing for me. I cannot, I really cannot describe what that did to my insides and to my head. I thought: I'm being educated finally.

And I realized that my deprivation had been stark. It occurred to me at that time that I should have had experiences earlier than that when I had to think through things and reason and defend my positions, and yet I had not had those experiences, even though I had four years of undergraduate training at TSU. I realized that the best training available in an all-black instant university was not equal to the best training one developed as a white university student. Separate was not equal; it just wasn't. No matter what kind of face you put on it or how many frills you attached to it, separate was not equal. I was doing sixteen years of remedial work in thinking.

So I worked my tail to the bone until it was time to go home at the end of the school year. I told my father that I had struggled up there, and that I hadn't been home in nine months, and I was kind of in a hurry, so he paid for me to fly home on Eastern Airlines. And that became a pattern with us.

That was my first plane trip, and I concentrated all the day before on not getting sick; I thought it would be embarrassing to get sick. I wondered how it would feel up there, if you could tell you were really in the air. I had on a navy-blue Lilli Ann suit which I bought in Boston, very expensive—which I had paid out of my allowance and gift money—because I wanted to make a good impression when I got home. It had a blue-and-white stand-up collar, and I had a big yellow wide-brimmed hat. And on the plane I recited the Lord's Prayer as it sped down the runway, holding my breath, not prepared at all for that feeling of movement. It was not like any conveyance I had ever been on.

There I was greeting my family in the Houston airport in my new suit and my yellow hat, and I did not know whether I had flunked out of Boston University Law School or not. And when I got off the plane, Houston looked very different to me. It was so flat. I couldn't get oriented to the flatness. At home on Campbell Street the ceiling was so low I said: "Why is this ceiling so low? It's closing in on us."

The grades were due to arrive in the mail at home. And every day my father was asking me: "Well, how was it?" And I would say: "Well, it was tough. It was really rough." That was so he wouldn't be surprised if I didn't make it. I was trying to prepare him for the worst. After I had been home a couple of weeks, I started to watch for the mail, to meet the mailman at the door. And one fine day a little envelope arrived. I took the envelope, crushed it in my hand, not telling anybody what had come, and went to the furthest room in the house, the back room, my folks' room, and, whispering a little prayer, closed the door and opened the envelope. Five little cards.

Now, they had to average 75 for me to make it. The first three were all above 75, they were nicely above 75. Then that one card, Procedure, a 70. All right, my heart fluttered just a little bit, but it looked as if the other grades were enough to help it out. And then I got to the last one and it was an 80 something. That was Commercial Law, bills and notes. Deep sigh of relief. So that was that. I said: "One year down, two to go." And of course my folks did not understand what I had been going through.

It was better from then on. I still had to work, but I didn't worry about punching out. I thought: If I can survive the first year, I'll make it the rest of the way. So after that, things loosened up a little.

One day, after I was back at school for my second year, I was floored when a Wills professor came up to me and asked me to come by his office after class. I did and he said: "I think you have some potential as a lawyer. I want you to go talk to Ed Brooke, who is a lawyer in Boston." And he gave me a little card which said Brooke's office was at 10 Pemberton Square. I did go see Brooke, but it didn't lead to anything. The point was that here was a professor who had said to me that I was finally on top of the thing.

Sometimes we would have parties at Bill Gibson's. We would tap on his window, which was at sidewalk level, and he would come around to the back and let us in. Bill always took care to have a nice place because when he first came to law school he had looked for a place in the West End and been refused by the person renting the rooms, who said: "We don't want no niggers here." Bill used to tell us about the topless and bottomless dancers and the twenty-five-cent teaser. I don't know about that, but he was always not riding the subway to save his money for such adventures.

One other thing I made time for that second year was chapel. As long as I was with my family, religion had remained in the mode of prohibition. It did not become liberating for me until I got out from under the careful watch of the Reverend B. M. Jordan and the Deacon Charles Jordan. I had to fit into their mold as long as I was at home. Even though I didn't always abide by the Covenant of the Baptist Church, every time I violated that code I felt guilty about it. I felt guilty because I wasn't sure it was all right for me to go out and have a few beers and party all night. I would do that, but then I would say: "I must ask forgiveness for that." Then I'd do it again, and then I'd repent again. I went through that pattern until I went to Boston.

Here I was by myself in Boston, Massachusetts, thousands of miles away from Campbell Street and the Reverend, and I said: "You know you don't have to go to church if you don't want to." But then I found that I wanted to. I wanted to go to chapel, and I went practically every Sunday.

And the minister there, Howard Thurman, was outstanding. He would have a message on the back of the chapel program and it was always something moving and meaningful, and I thought: You know, it is really not necessary to adhere to this ritual of prohibition. God really is caring. He wants me to live according to the preachments of His scripture, but He doesn't mean for me to be hounded into heaven. He just wants me to live right and treat other people right. I decided that then, and it was very comforting.

In contrast to the messages at home, Howard Thurman focused on how we walked around every day; he did not try to get us to live because of the great lure of something beyond. His sermons were focused on the present time that all of us were having difficulty coming to grips with. I would carry that program home and often preach his sermons to my roommates once I got back, whether they wanted to hear them or not. I was making sure I had it all. If I could preach it again, I really did have it. Of course my roommates didn't want to hear it, but that didn't make any difference to me. I saved every chapel program from my time up there.

Howard Thurman's messages made so much sense to me that at one point I thought: Well, maybe I ought to go into theology rather than law. And I remember writing my father: "Well, I might shift to theology out of law." And of course my father was just ecstatic about that. He called to say he was so excited about it, that he saw it as my following in the footsteps of his mother, Mary Jordan, who was a missionary. When he said that, that sobered me. I knew that what he had in mind was not what I had in mind. So that was just a brief period.

Then it was the end of my third year, and I told my father for them not to plan on the expense of coming up for commencement until he heard from me. My time in law school had been an overwhelming financial burden on him and on Bennie and Rose Mary. It had been a financial burden for all of them. And Rose Mary got married to John McGowan and there had been that expense.

But when I went by the office and got the computation that said that I was a law school graduate, when it was definite that I was going to make it, I called home, and my father just couldn't wait. When I gave him the word to come, he went out and purchased a 1959 Oldsmobile 98. Black, spanking, brand-new Olds 98, as long as a city block, to drive to Boston. They all loaded up to come: my mother and my father and Bennie and Rose Mary.

I arranged for them to stay at Charlesgate, and they decided to spend some additional time in Boston, so it was a big occasion. They came to the hooding ceremony, and then to the commencement at Boston Garden. Issie and I were the only women who had started in the class who were graduating and I told my father: "You won't be able to see us because the graduates are in the thousands, but we'll be there. I'll be there." But it turned out the law school graduates got to walk across the stage to get their degrees. I couldn't wait to get that scroll, tied with a little red ribbon, back to my room, and open it to make sure that it was really a law degree from Boston University. But that's what it was. And I sat down and cried. I thought: Well, you've done it. You've really done it.

Then we all went out and had a celebration—and we were a long way from the low ceiling on Campbell Street.

5. HOUSTON

In the summer of 1961, on a sultry, sticky day in late August, Bennie married old Houstonian Ben Creswell, at the house on Campbell Street. It was like old times, like Sunday mornings long ago. The Reverend Lucas of Good Hope Missionary Baptist Church officiated. The pianist played "Oh, Promise Me." Rose Mary stood as matron of honor; Creswell's brother Nehemiah stood as best man. Ben Jordan gave his second daughter away.

In a curved archway massed with flowers, Bennie repeated her vows—gowned in a waltz-length white chiffon with pink embroidered insets, veiled by a tiered headpiece set with rhinestones.

Barbara, just back from a summer teaching at Tuskegee, felt she had nothing new and special to wear for Bennie's big day, nothing befitting the sister of the bride, nothing fancy enough. Settling on a beige shirtwaist she had had for years, she felt unprepared for the moving on of this sister she had followed around for so long.

In the two years since her return from Boston, she had

leaned on the old patterns of Wheatley high school days. She had lived at home with her parents, had gone with Bennie and hairdresser Wilma Brown, their friend from Sharon Street days, to their special hangout for late-night music and drinks. The three of them going Dutch, as money was still tight, though not as tight as during summers home from law school.

In the spring Barbara had decided that she could not continue to operate an office from the pink-and-green dining room on Campbell, and had applied to six schools to teach a summer government course, to save money for a place of her own. Tuskegee invited her to come. "I hoped you would do more with your law degree than that," her father told her, disappointed at her going back in time to teach at his old school. "I plan to," she assured him.

Saving every penny she made, she had deposited it all, on her return, in the Bank of the Southwest and set out to locate a space. An old acquaintance from Wheatley days, Asbury Butler, said he was looking at an office to share on Lyons Avenue, across the street from the grocery store of "old man Charles White," father of the Charles White who used to walk home from school with Barbara and the gang.

This large space was essentially one room, with no partitions, so that the two of them could divide it up to suit them. With Charles White Senior's help, they constructed three offices within this shell, one for each of them, and one for some prospective third lawyer who could share the seventy-dollars-a-month rent.

Until they could afford to hire a full-time secretary to sit in the common corridor fronting the offices, Barbara continued to use Valerie Lewis, who had been on the TSU yearbook staff when she had been editor. "She said she would help me out whenever I needed help, so I used her for petitions and wills, whatever I needed to have typed."

To insure that her father felt that she was setting out to fully use the education he had paid for, she invited him down to see the place. "I said to my father: 'I'm ready to open this office on Lyons Avenue, and I have to furnish it.' He came up and looked at it. Then he took me to Aaran Used Office Furniture, where I picked out the things for this new office. I got a white formica desk with black trim —black and white were always my favorite colors—and a secondhand white leather desk chair, one of those swivel chairs, with a lower back than I would have liked. Then I said: 'All right, I need some chairs for the clients to sit in.' And we found two little squatty cream-colored chairs. I would have preferred white, but there weren't any white, so I got those. And a file cabinet. And I selected all that and paid whatever it cost and got a date of delivery.

"And then I told my father: 'Well, I've got these items of furniture, but there's no heat in the office.' My father came back up to see the space. 'I'll buy you a heater,' he said. And he bought a little metal-covered gas heater and we connected it to a gas jet, and that kept the office warm. And he thought it was fine to do this."

But then, with her furniture in place and her rent paid, Barbara found herself with time on her hands. With Bennie gone, things didn't feel the same.

Things were not the same in the city either. Downtown the Houston newspapers reflected the white community's efforts to contain black mobility; in the Fifth Ward, schoolchildren took their right to cross the tracks into the courtroom.

The day of Bennie's wedding (August 16, 1961) the

Houston *Post* ran a drama notice about a new play at the Alley Theatre. "At a time when it faces great peril again, this nation is observing the centennial of the war that unified it at terrible cost. There is no strict theatre vehicle suitable to that purpose. But Stephen Vincent Benét's epic poem 'John Brown's Body,' as adapted for stage use, is the greatly acceptable answer."

In the state capitol in Austin, the House General Investigation Committee charged that the National Association for the Advancement of Colored People had flagrantly violated a 1957 injunction which prohibited their encouraging or financing lawsuits in which they had no direct interest. The *Post* that day quoted: "Violation of the permanent injunction . . . not only is clearly established but such violations have been so flagrant and highly publicized that it would appear that those officials charged with protecting the legal rights of the people of Texas would have become aware of these violations and challenged the unlawful activities of the NAACP.

"It is the responsibility of the office of the attorney general of the State of Texas to keep alert for indications through any and all channels, including the daily press and NAACP publications, as to any violations of the injunction against the NAACP.

"Likewise, citizens of Texas must be alert to possible agitators and those who would stir up trouble among races that have lived together in comparative peace and friendship for nearly a century."

Also stirring up trouble, for the last five years, had been students in all-black schools, such as those in the Fifth Ward, who tried in vain to get the *Brown* decision put into effect locally.

In the fall of 1956, Mamie Reed Lee had accompanied

Beneva Williams, a fourteen-year-old student at E. O.
Smith Junior High, to meet with the attorney of the Houston Independent School District. "When all this came
about she was in my homeroom. I would take the rollbook
and provide the records for them—such as, I testified that
she lived right across the track from McReynolds, a white
school. Beneva was a very smart student. She later went to
Rusk and the University of California for degrees in soci-
ology. She was quite a knowledgeable little girl, and ambitious. That's why her parents wanted her to get the fullest
benefit from her education.

"But there was all kinds of irreverent stuff going on to
circumvent these transfers. The School Board and their
lawyer were as against the idea as anyone could be. They
scampered around any way they could to prevent any
black child from attending a white school. They would use
all types of wording to keep from implementing the decision. That lawyer was somebody to be long remembered—
honey, I couldn't tell you all the things he did."

Williams and another student brought suit against the
Houston Independent School District, but the District
Court, in an unreported opinion, issued only a general
order to the School Board to desegregate its schools "with
all deliberate speed." Which meant they continued to do
nothing.

Four years later, taking note of this inaction, the Court
found that HISD's nonspecific plan for desegregation in no
way complied with the Court's orders, "nor does it constitute a good faith attempt at compliance," but rather, "a
subterfuge designed only to accomplish further evasion
and delay." To remedy that, the Court set out its own
plan: a stair-step proposal which prescribed that the
schools desegregate the first grade in 1960, and add a suc-

cessively higher grade each year until complete desegregation was accomplished: a gradual method, which the judge called "a virtuous plan by which young children, free of predilections, adapt themselves to circumstances which might be disturbing to their elders."

That year, a first-grader tried to transfer to a white school. Delois Ross, represented by her mother, brought suit claiming that she had been discriminated against when a school she applied to refused her admission on the grounds that its first-grade class was already filled to capacity. But the appellate court did not find that this was an intentional act of discrimination, and gave the schools another extension of time to make the new plan work.

Two years later, Ross (now referred to in court records as Delores) tried again, bringing a suit which called into question the longstanding "brother-sister" rule, which said that a child must attend the same school as any older sibling.

In 1962, in *Ross* v. *Dyer*, the U. S. Fifth Circuit Court of Appeals finally took a long look at the whole mess in Houston. "The Houston Independent School District, one of the nation's largest in terms of scholastics and up to 1960 the largest segregated school system in the country, had approximately 190,000 students enrolled at the time the Judge heard this matter . . .

"Following the traditional pattern of Southern schools, the whole system was segregated. This was not the result of spurious gerrymandering. It is open and frank. Separate zones for white children and Negroes were—and are still— maintained. Every geographical area within the system is therefore simultaneously in two zones, one for Negroes and one for whites."

The Court pointed out that under their stair-step plan

only twelve blacks had been admitted to all-white schools in 1960, only thirty-three in 1961, and that, to make matters worse, the District Judge, in holding against Ross in his lower court, obviously thought Houston was doing just fine: ". . . evidence shows that the transition has been accomplished thus far in an orderly manner, with no destruction of the school curriculum, and with a minimum of friction and discontent . . . a matter in which the City of Houston may well take pride."

In light of this long obfuscation, the Court declared that the HISD's use of the old brother-sister plan was indeed another attempt to block integration, stating that it could only "bring about the rankest sort of discrimination as between Negro children living side by side in the same neighborhood."

Overruling the lower court's argument that the rule applied equally to white students, they said: "[W]e think that logic alone is insufficient to overcome the practical effect of this rule which as to some Negro families perpetuates a segregated system despite the plain purpose of the stair-step plan to ameliorate it. . . .

"No prior decision of this Court . . . affords any basis for thinking that a stair-step plan with that built-in condition would merit judicial approval."

Change continued to be incredibly slow. Barbara felt that from the time of the *Brown* decision to the *Ross* case nothing had happened. The only way to move things along, she concluded, was to get in a position where you could implement the laws. So, for the first time, she began to think seriously about politics.

Mamie's husband—handsome, urbane businessman Wilmer Lee—set himself up as the one to help her get started. "You got to know the kingpins, the people who are influential in the political arena. Because if you're not in the right place at the right time, it doesn't matter what your credentials are. She had a good background, but she didn't know the people. You've got to have connections. You've got to get into the smoke-filled rooms in the back. I showed her the ropes," he reminisced. "I've thought and thought about any other way she could have made it where she is. But that was the way to do it back then."

Wilmer introduced her to his best connections. While she was home from Boston, he had taken her to meet prominent black millionaire Hobart Taylor, Sr., at that time owner of the taxi franchise for the city. (If you wanted a taxi permit you had to get it from Hobart Taylor.) Barbara was presented as a comer, a new face, a law student at Boston University. Taylor received her in his plush home surrounded by the most respected representatives of the anti-establishment coalition of that time—labor, minorities, old-line white liberals. Explaining that his own son had graduated from Michigan's law school, he took her into his confidence and instructed her in the ways of power. To get control of the party you had to contribute money to it. For example, he had given thousands in support of the conservative governor, John Connally.

But neither Uncle Wilmer nor the liberal coalition was to get Barbara elected to public office. It was not their style to win. They preferred the role of rock in the shoe or burr on the saddle of the powers that be. From time to time they ran one or two successful candidates in statewide races against the moneyed conservatives. (One such was State Representative Bob Eckhardt, for whose success Wilmer also took credit. "I remember when they were going around asking me if I could get Bob somewhere to speak, let him get exposure, and I found him a spot on the program at Burris School. That was his first notice.") From time to time the liberals seized rare local spots, such as placing the first black woman on the Houston School Board.

But the feeling among them remained that if you were in, it meant you had sold out. The mood, the credo, of the inner circle of the Harris County Democrats then could be summed up in the words attributed to longtime liberal spokeswoman Billie Carr:

"It's not always a matter of winning; there's nothing wrong with losing."

■

After I got my law degree I really wanted to stay in Boston. It was the whole integration thing; that was just it. I thought: The air is freer up here. I'll stay here and not go back to Texas. I had that idea in my head. I thought: The opportunities must be greater up here and I won't have all the hangups with segregation. I'll just stay. Having said that, I took the Massachusetts bar exam. While I made these decisions and studied for the exam, I served as a housemother at one of the dorms.

Having decided I wanted to stay, the next step was that I should look for a job. Which I did. I went to a couple of insurance companies. I didn't go to any lawyers because I didn't know any except Ed Brooke, and I had had one meeting with him in which he did not seem interested in advancing my future.

I could have gotten a job at John Hancock Insurance Company as one of the hundreds of lawyers they have doing various claims and things. But when the personnel person said that I could have a job and took me down the hall to show me the office I could have, it was one of a row of little cubbyholes all divided by plywood. So I thanked him very much and left. This required some reconsideration. I thought: Now, look—true the air is freer up here, true the opportunities are probably greater, but nobody in Boston, Massachusetts, is interested in the advancement of Barbara Jordan. They don't know you. They don't even know your name. I decided: Maybe it makes more sense to go home where people will be interested in helping you.

So at that point I called my mother and said: "I'm coming home." And she said: "Thank God." She said: "I've been praying every night that you would decide to come home. When I got down on my knees I knew that you couldn't really stay up there." "Well," I told her, "I didn't know I had all that working against me when I was doing my best to stay."

So I got organized and came back home. On my return from Boston to Texas my father purchased a Simca for me, a light-green Simca, a little car. The understanding between us was that he would pay on the note until I could afford to do it myself. So I was driving this little Simca around and one day my father said to me: "Okay, now you've got the law degree from Boston University. What next?"

And I asked myself: "What next?" I said: "You're a lawyer. The first order of business is that you ought to pass the Texas bar, because it doesn't help at all if you are not licensed to practice in Texas." I took a bar review course for the bar exam, and the administering officials and I had a little dispute as to whether I was a resident of Massachusetts, as I had taken that bar exam, or whether I was a resident of Texas. But when I was called before these gentlemen to talk about my residency, I just told them I had never intended to stay in Boston. That it was a matter of formality to take the bar exam in the state in which you had graduated from law school. I told them: "I have always been a Texan."

The Texas bar exam was a three-day affair. And after the second day, when I really felt I was doing well on it, I got a call from the dorm in Boston saying that I had passed the Massachusetts bar. So I announced this to all of my friends who were assembled in the motel on East Eleventh in Austin, where we were staying while taking the bar. I told them: "Well, now, folks, I'll have you know there is one in your midst who is already a lawyer." And that required our having to go out and celebrate my passing the Massachusetts bar when we should have been studying for the third day of exams. I said: "This makes me a Boston lawyer." Then Andrew Jefferson, who graduated from the University of Texas Law School and was also taking the bar, said: "That's almost as good as being a Philadelphia lawyer." So we all had a good time.

I passed the Texas bar also, and the question still was: "What next?" I thought: I'll just have some cards printed up saying BARBARA JORDAN, ATTORNEY AT LAW. And I'll hand them out at Good Hope and to anybody who'll take them. Then, if anybody calls wanting me to do something, I'll do it.

I was still at my family's house at that time when I started handing out my lawyer's cards. And then people did start asking me to do things for them as an attorney, so that I was working out of the dining room at Campbell Street and driving the little Simca to the courthouse. But my problem had not been solved. I had passed two bar exams, but I did not have that much to do really. I asked myself: "What does one do after work with one's free time?"

The campaign of John Kennedy for President and Lyndon Johnson for Vice President was under way. I was interested in their getting elected, so I went down to the Harris County Democratic Headquarters and offered my services. I asked: "Is there anything I can do to be of assistance in getting John Kennedy and Lyndon Johnson elected President and Vice President of the United States?" And the people there said: "Well, what do you want to do?" "I'll do anything," I told them. "I've got lots of time."

I started then to help with the development of a blockworker program for the forty black and predominantly black precincts in Harris County. There was a lady named Versie Shelton and a man named John Butler who designed the program, which was headed by Chris Dixie, a labor lawyer and a liberal Democrat. We four keyed the whole operation so that there would be one block worker per twenty houses in these forty precincts. That campaign, our block-worker effort, was eminently successful. Of the forty boxes in those precincts we worked, there was a turnout of some eighty per cent of the vote. It was the most successful get-out-the-vote that anybody could recall in Harris County.

I continued to work with Chris Dixie and Versie Shelton and John Butler. We went from church to school to meetinghouse, everywhere we were invited, selling the blockworker program. Then one night Versie Shelton could not attend one of the meetings in Fifth Ward to give the speech which she always gave, the presentation, so I substituted for her. And after that speech Chris Dixie and John

Butler decided that it was a waste of time for me to lick stamps and address envelopes and be an all-around generalist. They decided that I ought to be put on the speech-making circuit for the Harris County Democrats.

And that's what I did. I spoke primarily to black groups, political groups, civic organizations, clubs, and churches. Any group could call who needed a speaker, and I would go. I was not restricted to black groups, but of course all of the white groups were of a liberal bent. If you called the Harris County Democrats requesting a speaker, you were naturally a liberal.

By the time the Kennedy-Johnson campaign ended successfully, I had really been bitten by the political bug. My interest, which had been latent, was sparked. I think it had always been there, but that I did not focus on it before because there were certain things I had to get out of the way before I could concentrate on any political effort. I recall I had been keenly interested in the Stevenson-Eisenhower contest, but my interest had been unfocused. Now that I was thinking in terms of myself, I couldn't turn politics loose.

So I continued to speak: To any group who wanted me, on any topic they requested. If they wanted somebody to talk about flowers, I'd be the one out there to talk about flowers. And there were numerous requests. I was getting my name in the paper often at this point, as there was the novelty of my being a black woman lawyer, and graduating from a law school in Boston, and sounding different. That got attention.

After the presidential race I remained active with the Harris County Democrats and we began to screen candidates for various local offices. By that time I had left Campbell Street and was settled in my office on Lyons Avenue, when one day Chris Dixie said to me that I ought to run for the Texas House of Representatives when that election came up again in 1962. Dixie was the one I worked with most closely on this whole political scene, so when he broached that matter I paid attention.

I said: "Well, Chris, I make enough money to eat and buy my clothes, and gasoline for my little Simca, but I certainly don't make enough money to run a political race." I told him that. I said: "I don't have the money." But he said: "Don't worry about that. The filing fee is five hundred dollars and I'll lend you the money for a filing fee. You can pay me back." So, all right, Chris loaned me the five hundred dollars. Five crisp new one-hundred-dollar bills. And I liked that.

I thought: I've got to get serious about this. I've been talking politics, and wanting to get into it, and here I am. I asked myself: "Do you really understand the way Texas state government functions?" The answer being no, I went out and got a state government textbook and read it. I read about all the various funds, the special funds, when the legislature met, and how often—the rules of the game. Or what I thought at that point were the rules of the game in the state of Texas.

I don't remember in which era of Texas government it was, but some governor talked about *retrenchment* and *reform*, and I liked the sound of those words. I thought: Now here, these are two nice, fine words. I thought about them, and I decided: "That will be my campaign theme. Retrenchment and reform." And I began to work them into my campaign speeches after I had announced for the House of Representatives.

There were twelve state representatives coming from Harris County, all running at large, so that we all had to canvass the whole county. The Harris County Democrats advanced their slate of candidates for the state legislature, and I was one of these, and each of us had as an opponent a conservative, backed by other groups. My opponent in the race was Willis Whatley, a lawyer also.

We were all presented to a big gathering of liberal Democrats from Harris County, twelve of us, including me and Bob Eckhardt. Each candidate was presented and said a few words, and I was the tenth candidate to get up and give a speech. I gave them my Retrenchment and Reform, and talked about all the good things I was going to do in Texas state government if I got elected, the text-book type of concerns, such as how I was going to break up the University Fund, and change the state budgeting procedures. I talked a lot about welfare, and how we had the obligation to take care of people who couldn't take care of themselves. I thought it all sounded wonderful.

At the conclusion of my speech the audience stood up and applauded. That was the first standing ovation I had ever received, and it occurred to me right then that the question was: Why are all these people standing? They hadn't stood for the others. I needed to know whether they were standing because I was the only black, or the only woman, or sounded different, or had said such fantastic things about state reform. I didn't know what had really turned them on, what had given them the spark. And I needed to know so that I could keep doing it throughout my campaign. There they were, all on their feet just cheering and cheering. And after that response the last two speakers, whoever they were, Places Eleven and Twelve, were just wiped out.

From that time on, as we moved along on the campaign trail, the standing joke was: "Let's get there early so we can get on the program before Barbara Jordan." That was when I first started to hear that.

Meanwhile Hobart Taylor, Sr., had contributed twenty-five dollars to my campaign to let me know he was behind me. And Chris Dixie continued to keep me pumped up. They set me up to go around to the Houston *Post* and the *Chronicle* and ask for their endorsements, which of course I did not get. But Chris continued to say: "You're great. You're going to win." He had compiled all the figures: "You're going to get ninety per cent of the black vote, thirty per cent of the white vote. There's no way you can lose."

On occasions when I would be at the same meetings with my opponent, Willis Whatley, I would listen to him and I would say to myself: "Anybody in his right mind will vote for me against this fellow." I would think: Because I've got a better case to present. I'd look at him and I'd just shake my head, thinking: You ought to just forget it, Willis, and go back to the practice of law.

So one fine day Election Day came. And I cast my vote at seven o'clock in the morning. The polling place was filled by seven o'clock there in Fifth Ward, and I got reports that it was that way at all the black boxes in the city.

The Atlanta Life Insurance Company had let me have a headquarters downtown in their building on Prairie Street, free for the campaign. And people were pouring in there for the returns. As the first returns showed up on the television, I, of course, was behind. But Chris kept telling me: "Just wait until after ten o'clock when the black boxes come in." But they came in and I still hadn't won. Reality

entered. I got forty-six thousand votes, and Willis Whatley got sixty-five thousand. And that was that.

I asked myself: "What happened?" It was all supposed
to work out. Bob Eckhardt won. Now, Eckhardt was an
incumbent; but Whatley was not. Others were not. And I
got the feeling that everybody won on the slate endorsed
by the Harris County Democrats but me.

I asked; "How could everybody else do so well? How
could the other liberals make it and not me?" I did well in
the black areas, but I didn't do well anywhere else. The
feeling I had was that I had been used to get black people
to vote. And that nobody else on the ticket brought that
kind of strength to me in return. Those fine people, I
thought, all the Harris County Democrats, they had me
come to teas and coffees in their areas in the southwest part
of town, and the people would come to hear me and be
very polite. But they didn't give me their votes. The votes
were just not there from these fine white people. That was
very puzzling to me, and disturbing. I spent a lot of time
trying to figure out what did happen in that race.

Chris Dixie was not bothered. He said: "That was your
first race, and even though a lot of people voted for you,
and you got around a lot, there were a lot of people who
didn't know you and didn't know who you were. You
have to give some weight to your being a newcomer." But
a professor at Rice University who came into my campaign
headquarters during that first race had said to me: "You
know it's going to be hard for you to win a seat in the
Texas Legislature. You've got too much going against you:
You're black, you're a woman, and you're large. People
don't really like that image." "Well," I told him, "I can't

do anything about the first two elements." But I had tucked that away, as something to remember. At the time I did not feel those were factors which had to be overcome. I felt that the *black* and the *woman* stuff were just side issues, and that people were going to ignore that. Now, that was naïveté on my part, but it seemed to me that no one would care at all about such factors, that those were extraneous issues, that they were neutral.

After the primary I continued to go around and speak and meet people and testify before committees in the Texas Legislature on pending educational bills that would benefit blacks. All that whole bit in order to get my name well-known. One day I went to Austin to testify, and when I sat up in the House gallery and looked down at Willis Whatley at his desk, I thought, "I ought to be in his place. I deserve it."

Then it was time to run again in 1964, and I hoped things would be different. This time there was another seat where the incumbent was more vulnerable than Willis Whatley, so I thought: I'll try for that place instead. But John Ray Harrison—a white who had been a part of that original slate of twelve candidates, and I guess had also lost —wanted to run for that better seat.

One day he called me to his office and explained that it would make better sense for me to go again for the same place, Place Ten, against the same opponent that I had before. He made me feel that it was the thing to do, so I agreed to that. But I remember thinking after I left him that Harrison had sold me a bill of goods, and that I had made a mistake in not saying: "I'm going against this guy who is more vulnerable." I knew that, and I took a deep breath and said to myself: "Well, you made a mistake."

Willis Whatley, now the incumbent, had his big billboards all over the county, and his conservative groups behind him. So we had a repeat performance.

When I saw that the second race was an extension of the first, and that Whatley had won, and that John Ray Harrison had also won, but I had not, I didn't go to the campaign headquarters. Instead, I just got in my car and drove around most of election night. The question was: "Is a seat in the state legislature worth continuing to try for?" I got a few thousand more votes the second time out, but the basic facts were the same. I asked myself: "Am I just butting my head against something that's absolutely impossible to pull off?" I drove around in the car, listening to the returns while I asked myself: "Why are you doing this?"

After I got home and had gone to bed, my campaign manager and campaign co-ordinator came to my house asking: "Where have you been? The people are all waiting for you at headquarters." I said: "I've been driving around." And when Chris called to say, "Well, we've got the analysis for you," I snapped at him, "I've got the analysis for you: I didn't win." And went back to bed.

I had to decide by myself whether I was going to stick it out a little longer, and thinking that if I did I certainly couldn't do it in concert with anybody else. I couldn't let anyone else get in my head and make my decisions any more. I wasn't going to go to their teas if they were not voting for me at their polls.

The first order of business was to decide: Is politics worth staying in for me?

Meanwhile, my family and my friends out there started in on the refrain that if I was not going to be winning, I ought to want to get married. And I remembered what the Rice professor had said, and realized that different standards were applied to men like John Ray Harrison and Willis Whatley than were going to be applied to me. At that time, I finally admitted that fact.

Public expectations were different for a white man than for a black woman. Where a man was concerned, the public perception was that he was supposed to get out there and lead and do and make decisions and the rest of it; and no one said to him that he needed to care for the babies, or iron the curtains, or clean the johns. That was not expected of him. What was expected was that he'd marry a woman to do it for him. And why not?

The public believed that a woman had to have, over and above and beyond other aspirations, a home and family. That was what every normal woman was supposed to want. And any woman who didn't want that was considered something a little abnormal. People didn't expect a woman to make rough decisions. She was the ward of her man; she was always to be available at her husband's side no matter where he had to go or what he had to do. She must always be prepared to turn and kiss his puckered lips.

Now, I thought it unfortunate that the public perceived such a neat little box for us, and that in most cases we felt that the box was right. I thought: The question you have to decide, Barbara Jordan, is whether you're going to fly in the face of what everybody expects out there because you've got your eye someplace else, or whether you can bring the public along to understand that there are some women for whom other expectations are possible.

I realized that my friends out there thought that marriage was the most important thing there was, and that they all wanted to guarantee that they got the right man and the right home. I ticked them off in my head, all the people I went to school with—Rose Mary and Bennie and the Justices—and I thought: "Now they've already done that and they expect me to do that." My mother wanted me to be married, and my father wanted me to be married, and so did everybody else. But they also wanted me to be successful. I decided I would tell them: "Down the road a piece." In those years I always said: "Down the road a piece. Just let me get it all organized, and then we'll see."

But I made the decision, and it was a fairly conscious one, that I couldn't have it both ways. And that politics was the most important thing to me. I reasoned that this political thing was so total in terms of focus that, if I formed an attachment over here, this total commitment would become less than total. And I didn't want that. I did not want anything to take away from the singleness of my focus at that time.

I had learned that five crisp one-hundred-dollar bills and talking about doing away with the University Fund was not the way to win. And, as I had learned back in the Elks Oratorical Contest, I did not like losing. I intended to devote my full attention to figuring out the way to succeed. And the first thing I knew was that it was not to let anybody else get inside my head. It was not to let anybody else make the decisions again.

■

Barbara ended her second race obsessed with the idea that she had been the only loser in a slate of white liberals who had sailed to victory on the strength of her speaking voice and her black supporters. Had she studied the overall returns, however, she would have found that such endorsements as the Harris County Democrats guaranteed few victories for anyone. Their candidates served as irritants, but never threats, to the men who ran and would continue to run the state of Texas.

In her first election, the liberal coalition had presented a slate of twenty-four candidates for statewide offices from Governor to Democratic County Chairman. Sixteen of these lost; eight won primarily on the strength of being well-known and incumbents, or unopposed: the Commissioner of Agriculture, a state senator, a county judge, the county chairman. Of the twelve state representatives endorsed with Barbara, eight lost. Of the four who won, Bob Eckhardt, an incumbent, was the only victor, campaigning at large from the million-plus population of Harris County, who did not require a runoff election.

The black newspaper *Forward Times* (May 12, 1962) carried this assessment of her loss:

"A CHECK of the vote totals in predominantly Negro precincts show an estimated 24,000 Negroes spoke their piece at the polls Saturday.

"ATTORNEY BARBARA JORDAN, youthful Houstonian, in her first political test [received] slightly less than 23,000 of her 45,000 plus total vote in predominantly Negro precincts."

In her second race, a repetition of the first, Barbara refurbished her act, but she could not change the facts. She bought new clothes, suits with soft-colored bowed blouses; she traded in her faithful Simca—now worn down to the hubcaps, with its upholstery in tatters—for the first car she ever owned in her own name, a light-blue Cutlass from Bill McDavid Oldsmobile; she shared her voice with an even larger audience.

But none of these surface changes could alter Houston's white-dominated voting districts. The votes in the Fifth

Ward did not count equally with the votes in River Oaks. What it finally took to put Barbara in the state legislature was what it had always taken to open doors for her: the law. In these years an ever widening series of Supreme Court cases dealing with apportionment as a means of voter discrimination overlapped with legislation pushed by a new President from the Texas hill country who remembered how things had been when he was a poor boy from a rough countryside.

On March 26, 1962, the Supreme Court, commenting in *Baker* v. *Carr* on the Tennessee Legislature's failure to reapportion itself since 1901, ruled that a challenge to the make-up of a state legislature does not present a "political question" from which the courts must back away, rather that it does present a constitutional issue for which federal courts are empowered to fashion a judicial remedy. Although in this decision the justices evaded the question of redistricting to comply with the Fourteenth Amendment (Equal Protection), and said little about the relationship between legislative apportionment and equal protection, nonetheless it signaled the entrance of the federal courts into the arena of state legislative apportionment. Coming six weeks before Barbara's first race, it was an unnoted crack in the dike of white control.

A year later, in March 1963—the year of the light-blue Olds, and Barbara's push to begin campaigning for a second try—Justice Douglas, in *Gray* v. *Sanders*, articulated for the first time the concept of "one person, one vote," which would initiate the change that finally made possible black voting strength.

Finding that the Georgia county unit system, as used in state primary elections, violated the Fifteenth Amendment

(Right of Blacks to Vote), and the Nineteenth (Right of Women to Vote), Douglas said: "How then can one person be given twice or 10 times the voting power of another person in a statewide election merely because he lives in a rural area or because he lives in the smallest rural county? Once the geographical unit for which a representative is to be chosen is designated, all who participate in the election are to have an equal vote—whatever their race, whatever their sex, whatever their occupation, whatever their income, and wherever their home may be in that geographical unit. This is required by the Equal Protection Clause of the Fourteenth Amendment. The concept of 'we the people' under the Constitution visualizes no preferred class of voters but equality among those who meet the basic qualifications. The idea that every voter is equal to every other voter in his State, when he casts his ballot in favor of one of several competing candidates, underlies many of our decisions. . . . The conception of political equality from the Declaration of Independence, to Lincoln's Gettysburg Address, to the Fifteenth, Seventeenth, and Nineteenth Amendments can mean only one thing—one person, one vote."

These two cases reflected what Barbara had experienced in her own races: that black voters could help white liberals get elected, but could not represent themselves.

On November 22, 1963, the news flashed on television that the President of the United States had been shot down two hundred and fifty miles away in Dallas, Texas.

Visiting with Wilma Brown to get her hair done, Barbara was devastated. She stared at the screen and wept. "Kennedy will always be my President. If only I could have been that person instead of him; if I could only have let Oswald shoot me, my life would have been well worth it."

"You're crazy," Wilma allowed.

But the new, instant President, the accidental chief executive, Lyndon Johnson, had much more in common with her, and the country, than she could guess at the time. He knew that only those folks on the front of the bus also understood how it was for those on the back; that only the man who opens that back door can share the feelings of the man with hat in hand who has to come around to knock upon it. He had learned from a black staff member the trials of driving through the South from Washington to Texas, on a trip akin to Barbara's travels with Tom Freeman.

In the oval office, Johnson resolved to put an end to those shabby days. Picking up where Kennedy left off, the new President coaxed, bargained, and drove through the Congress an inclusive Civil Rights Act.

Principal among its sections were Equal Employment and Public Accommodations. Historically, the language and concepts of equal employment pertained only to government employees—in such vehicles as the Civil Service Rule of 1940—and, as there was no machinery established for enforcement, served only as expressions of policy.

The New Deal administration had sought to extend such hiring practices to all government contractors and all federal grants-in-aid programs, but, again, in the Unemployment Relief Act of 1933, there was no thought of extending this further, and there were no teeth to make it stick. In 1941, trying again, over substantial congressional opposition, FDR created the Fair Employment Practices Committee to encourage the employment of blacks in defense jobs. A second committee, set up two years later, again in the face of a balking Congress, tried to eliminate employment discrimination and promote full utilization of manpower in all training programs for war production and membership of labor unions. When it died also, that marked the end, for almost twenty years, of any attempt to force a policy of equal employment. Until, finally, Johnson guided through the Congress what became Title VII of the Civil Rights Act, making it unlawful to "fail or refuse to hire or to discharge any individual, or otherwise discriminate against any individual with respect to his compensations, terms, conditions, or privileges of employment, because of such individual's race, color, religion, sex, or national origin . . ."

Title II of the same bill, Injunctive Relief Against Discrimination in Places of Public Accommodations, echoed the language of the earliest attempts at civil rights legislation dating back to Emancipation and the Thirteenth Amendment.

In 1866, a civil rights act was passed declaring that all persons could own property and enter into contracts equally. In 1875, rights were extended further to include access to public facilities of all types. But in 1883 the Supreme Court, in a series of five cases referred to as "The Civil Rights Cases," held the laws unconstitutional because the Fourteenth Amendment could only restrict the abridgment of rights by states and not by individuals.

The majority opinion on the five cases, which concerned two plaintiffs who had been denied lodging, two who had been denied access to theaters, and one woman who was refused a seat in the ladies' railway compartment because she was of "African descent," argued:

"It may be . . . in the times when slavery prevailed the proprietors of inns and public conveyances were forbidden to receive persons of the African race, because it might assist slaves to escape from the control of their masters. This was merely a means of preventing such escapes, and was no part of servitude itself.

". . . The long existence of African slavery in this country gave us very distinct notions of what it was and what were its necessary incidents. Compulsory service of the slave for the benefit of the master, restraint of his movements except by the master's will, disability to hold property, to make contracts, to have a standing in court, to be a witness against a white person, and such like burdens and incapacities were the inseparable incidents of the institution.

". . . The only question under the present head, therefore, is, whether the refusal to any persons of the accommodations of an inn, or a public conveyance, or a place of public amusement, by an individual, and without any sanction or support from any state law or regulation, does inflict upon such persons any manner of servitude, or form of slavery, as those terms are understood in this country? Many wrongs may be obnoxious to the prohibitions of the fourteenth amendment which are not, in any just sense, incidents or elements of slavery.

". . . After giving to these questions all the consideration which their importance demands, we are forced to the conclusion that such an act of refusal has nothing to do with slavery or involuntary servitude.

". . . There were thousands of free colored people in this country before the abolition of slavery, enjoying all the essential rights of life, liberty, and property the same as white citizens; yet no one, at that time, thought that it was any invasion of their personal status as freemen because they were not admitted to all the privileges enjoyed by

white citizens or because they were subjected to discrim-
inations in the enjoyment of accommodations in inns, public conveyances, and places of amusement. Mere discrimination on account of race or color were not regarded as
badges of slavery."

Once again Justice John Marshall Harlan, a Kentucky
son of an earlier Supreme Court justice, entered a landmark dissent to the squashing of civil rights. This time,
eighty-one years ahead of the laws of the land, he argued:

"The purpose of the first section of the act of congress
of March 1, 1875, was to prevent *race* discrimination. It
does not assume to define the general conditions and limitations under which inns, public conveyances, and places of
public amusement may be conducted, but only declares
that such conditions and limitations, whatever they may
be, shall not be applied, by way of discrimination, on account of *race, color, or previous condition of servitude.*
The second section provides a penalty against any one denying, or aiding or inciting the denial, to any citizen that
equality of right given by the first section, except for
reasons of law applicable to citizens of every race or color,
and regardless of any previous condition of servitude.

". . . There seems to be no substantial difference between my brethren and myself as to what was the purpose
of congress; for they say what the essence of the law is, not
to declare broadly that all persons shall be entitled to the
full and equal enjoyment of the accommodations, advantages, facilities, and privileges of inns, public conveyances,
and theaters, but that such enjoyment shall not be subject
to any conditions applicable only to citizens of a particular race or color, or who have been in a previous condition
of servitude. . . .

"My brethren say that when a man has emerged from

slavery, and by the aid of beneficent legislation has shaken off the inseparable concomitants of that state, there must be some stage in the progress of his elevation when he takes the rank of a mere citizen, and ceases to be the special favorite of the laws, and when his rights as a citizen, or a man, are to be protected in the ordinary modes by which other men's rights are protected. It is, I submit, scarcely just to say that the colored race has been the special favorite of the laws. What the nation, through congress, has sought to accomplish in reference to that race is, what had already been done in every state in the Union for the white race, to secure and protect rights belonging to them as freemen and citizens; nothing more. The one underlying purpose of congressional legislation has been to enable the black race to take the rank of mere citizens. The difficulty has been to compel a recognition of their legal right to take that rank, and to secure the enjoyment of privileges belonging, under the law, to them as a component part of the people for whose welfare and happiness government is ordained. At every step in this direction the nation has been confronted with class tyranny . . ."

But this protest went unheard. It took President Lyndon Johnson to put into law the original language, almost verbatim, of the first civil rights act after Emancipation: "All persons within the jurisdiction of the U.S. shall be entitled to full and equal enjoyment of accommodations, advantages, facilities, and privileges of inns, public conveyances on land or water, theaters and other places of public amusement, applicable alike to citizens of every race and color regardless of any condition of servitude."

It had taken nine years from the cold, damp December day in Montgomery, Alabama, when Rosa Parks, a weary seamstress, had refused to give up her seat on a city bus to a white man, to bring about the end of segregated public transportation.

"Johnson's advocacy of the Civil Rights Act of 1964 was like the coming of all good things," Barbara said. "We were all startled, that this was really what he wanted to do, that this man in the White House was really going to push this. Governor John Connally was opposed to the public accommodations section, and I remember thinking that in terms of state politics this action on the part of this new President was going to be a real shocker to Texas."

But the climate throughout the South had changed enough to make Johnson's laws possible; and in June of 1964, one month after Barbara's second defeat, it permitted the Supreme Court to hand down six decisions that fleshed out and developed its guidelines for reapportioning state legislative bodies to conform with constitutional demands. These cases set forth the principle that the Constitution protects all citizens' rights to vote in state as well as federal elections, and put into effect the machinery which would change the voting outcome in Harris County.

In *Reynolds* v. *Sims* the Court held that the plaintiffs were denied equal protection by virtue of debasement of their votes because the Alabama Legislature had failed to reapportion itself. "The right to vote freely for the candidate of one's choice is of the essence of a democratic society, and any restrictions on that right strike at the heart of representative government. And the right of suffrage can be denied by a debasement or dilution of the weight of a citizen's exercise of the franchise."

In stating that legislative districting schemes which gave the same number of representatives to unequal numbers of constituents was as unconstitutional as imposing exclusive tests, gerrymandering to exclude certain voters, conducting all-white primaries, stuffing the ballot box, or altering the vote count, the Court declared: "One must be ever aware that the Constitution forbids sophisticated as well as simpleminded modes of discrimination."

Houston, as the country, had come a long way.

Finally, in *Wesberry* v. *Sanders*, the Court clarified that equal representation for equal numbers of people was the fundamental goal. Here, dealing with national elections, it did not base its holding on the Fourteenth Amendment, as it had for state elections, but rather decided that the language in the Constitution which stated that members of the U. S. House of Representatives shall be elected "by the People" meant, in historical context, that "as nearly as is practicable one man's vote in a congressional election is to be worth as much as another."

So, in 1965, with a great deal of protest reminiscent of earlier integration disputes, Harris County reapportioned its legislative districts, and Barbara found herself in the newly created Eleventh State Senatorial District, an area including the Fifth Ward, composed of 38 per cent blacks, a large block of Chicanos, and white laborers affiliated with the AFL-CIO.

It was the old liberal coalition; but this time, as she found out when she spread out a map on her desk to check the precincts in the new district, the votes counted differently. In 1962 and 1964 she had carried every single box in what was now the Eleventh District.

Since her last defeat she had been serving, from nine to five, as the administrative assistant to County Judge Bill Elliot; then heading back to Lyons Avenue to tend her own practice, from five to ten. She and Asbury had taken a third lawyer and hired a secretary, and she was putting money away in the bank with her two jobs.

Since the last race she had been asking herself: "How many more times are you going to run, Barbara?" Now, with the redistricting of Harris County, the answer was simple: "One more time."

In Bill Elliot's office that day, talking over with him the prospects of running against white, male Charlie Whitfield, a liberal legislator who had served eight years in the Senate already, she got a call from Charlie.

"Barbara," he asked after a friendly little prelude, "are you going to run for the new Senate seat?"

"Well, now, I'm not sure, Charlie. But I certainly am thinking about it."

"I thought I ought to let you know I'm going to run again," he said.

"Well, good luck, Charlie."

Hanging up, she reasoned aloud to Judge Elliot. If Charlie was getting a head start on this, she'd better quit her assistant's job and get on with it. "You could wait until the filing deadline," Elliot offered, but Barbara was ready to plunge into the race full time—now that the stakes had changed.

This time she did not wait on Chris Dixie's call. "Chris," she announced in his ear, "I'm going to run for the state Senate."

"Well," he hedged, "all right. All right."

"Chris, I understand that Charlie Whitfield is also running."

"Well, yes, Charlie came in and talked to me about that. I told him just to go on and do what he had to do."

"I just want it understood I'm going to run."

"Fine. Fine. You know we're with you."

But she was no surer of that than he was. Barbara Jordan had placed the Executive Committee of the Harris County Democrats in a turmoil. Charlie Whitfield was a good liberal, a staunch labor supporter; they had endorsed him every time he had run before, and he had always won his races. Barbara was their star, her speeches had brought them lots of votes; but she had lost both her early races.

Behind closed doors they battled it out in long, acrimonious arguments. "I never heard what happened in there," Barbara said. "But I heard they were highly uncomfortable about it."

What occurred in that secret meeting was that for the first time those factors cited as handicaps by the Rice professor had begun to work for Barbara instead of against her.

Bob Eckhardt gave this version of the caucus: "Whitfield had good credentials. It was a pretty hard choice to make. What it got down to was institutional fairness. We had a pretty good tripod after the 'one man, one vote' got put into effect: labor, blacks, liberals. My district included Fifth Ward; some of my strongest boxes were in that district. You couldn't expect blacks to be one part of that tripod without their having a leader of their own. We couldn't say: 'You ought to support us but we won't support you.' Black votes made the difference for her. That's what got her in—and it sort of ended Whitfield's career."

Barbara thought that decision was fine.

Whitfield was incensed. "I'll fight it on the floor of the general meeting. I'll fight to overturn the Committee recommendation and win it on the floor," he sent word.

"I'll be there," Barbara assured him.

So there they sat in the school auditorium where the Executive Committee presented its endorsements—white man, black woman. Whitfield presented his case: his years of experience, his voting record for the support of firemen's and policemen's pension funds, his bills for industrial safety and minimum wage, his name identification, his vote-getting power.

Barbara made her speech: "I ran a race in 1962. You endorsed me and I lost. I ran a race in 1964. You endorsed me and I lost. I want you to know I have no intention of being a three-time loser."

The audience erupted in applause, but this time it was not her rhetoric that won the point. As Eckhardt put it: "We had already rigged it."

So the campaign was on, and this time Barbara was not going to go around talking about retrenchment and reform and cutting the Permanent University Fund. She knew that you didn't do that in Texas. You just sold yourself; so she would sell Barbara Jordan. This time she didn't set up her headquarters downtown in the Atlanta Life Insurance Company, but upstairs in the True Level Lodge Building right there on Lyons Avenue—down the street from her office, in the Fifth Ward where her constituents lived. And this time she didn't send white liberals to make her contacts with the newspapers, but set up her own appointments with the *Post* and *Chronicle*, telling them: "If you know you can't bring yourself to endorse me, then consider not endorsing my opponent either—to which the *Post* agreed. This time she directed her own block work. Assisted by secretary Lestine Lakes, campaign manager Aloysius Wickliff, and sociologist Wilhelmina Perry, she sent out sample ballots to all the thirty-five thousand black voters in her district, showing how to vote for her.

Frantically Charlie Whitfield retaliated with a blanketing

of campaign flyers, headed WIN WITH WHITFIELD, protesting what he called the "black block vote":

"WHAT THIS RACE BOILS DOWN TO is simply this: Should we have a seat to satisfy a few or do we send an experienced, effective legislator to Austin to do the JOB? A group known as the Coalition Steering Committee, most of whom come from other parts of the county and do not live in the 11th Senatorial District, have bowed to the demands of a Negro group known as the Harris County Council of Organizations, which in turn demanded that a candidate from the 11th Senatorial District be a member of the Negro race. This demand was met by the Coalition's acquiescence and subsequently by endorsement of the various units of the Coalition. On the other side of the question was whether or not the Coalition and the Council of Organizations would stand by J. C. ('Charlie') Whitefield, who had served this county well (even in their own estimation) for over eight years.

"So this race points up the question, Shall we have a seat for a member of the NEGRO race or shall we consider other factors such as qualifications and experience in order to give Harris County its most effective voice in the 11th District? We must not have TRADE-OUTS."

Barbara seized on this and threw it back in his face. Pointing out to crowds that she had lived all her life in the Fifth Ward, and that he had moved to the Eleventh Senatorial District for the campaign, she pinned "Carpetbagger" on him at every turn. Flinging back the claim of a black block vote, she aroused her audiences with: "Look, don't tell us about black block votes. You know white folks have been block-voting for the past century. We don't have to apologize. Our time has come!"

But what each time brought thunderous applause, shouting and stomping, and a feeling that at last the tide had turned for them, was her standard finish:

"My opponent asks, 'CAN A WHITE MAN WIN?' And I say to you: 'NO. NOT THIS TIME. NOT . . . THIS . . . TIME . . . !'"

She beat him two to one—making nationwide news as the first black woman in the Texas Legislature, one of a small group of the first blacks elected in the South since Reconstruction.

This time she didn't have to wait until ten o'clock for the black boxes to come in; this time she didn't drive around in her car wondering what had gone wrong. Watching the returns on Campbell Street, she waited until the election was assured, then said to her father and mother: "All right, let's get dressed and get down to the True Level Lodge for a celebration. I've just wiped him out."

Down on Lyons Avenue the cars were jammed in the street, with people spilling out onto the sidewalk and leaning out of upstairs windows. When they saw her the scream went up: "HERE SHE COMES!" Headquarters was mobbed with cameras, mikes, news reporters, all jammed together waiting for a glimpse of her, for the sound of that now magic voice.

And Barbara thought: This the way it ought to be. I am going to stay in the Senate as long as I want to stay there. Nobody can stop me now.

On May 9, 1966, the New York *Times* ran a beaming photograph of Barbara Jordan, above a story datelined Austin, which read: "Two Negroes were nominated to the

My Grandfather Patten.

Grandpa Patten's wagon and mules.

This is me, between my sisters Bennie (left) and Rose Mary.

Here I am at age ten.

Phillis Wheatley High School Chapter of the National Honor Society. I was president (I'm in the front row, fourth from left). 1952. *(Provost Studio, Houston)*

Here I am with LBJ, at my Fund-raiser at the Rice Hotel in Houston, October 1971. *(Houston Chronicle photograph)*

With my parents, Arlyne and Ben Jordan, after I had won the Democratic primary election to Congress, May 1972. (*Houston Chronicle photograph*)

At the Good Hope Missionary Baptist Church, with my mother and the pastor. (*Photo by Moneta Sleet, Jr., Ebony Magazine*)

The Texas Congressional Delegati Washington, D.C., during my first ter This luncheon group has been meeti in the Speaker's dining room since t early days of Sam Rayburn. (*Photo Moneta Sleet, Jr., Ebony Magazine*)

The House Judiciary Committee Subcommittee is about to begin impeachment proceedings. *(Photo by Moneta Sleet, Jr., Ebony Magazine)*

President Ford signs the Voting Rights Bill, August 1975. *(Photo by Frank Johnston, Washington Post)*

Bob Strauss and I at the Democratic National Convention, Madison Square Garden, July 1976. *(Wide World Photos)*

With President Jimmy Carter. I was pleased to have a Democratic President at last. *(Photo courtesy Office of Photography, House of Representatives)*

Groundbreaking for the Barbara Jordan Technical Institute in Houston, February 1978. From left to right: Bennie's husband, Ben Creswell; Uncle Wilmer Lee; Aunt Mamie Reed Lee; my mother, Arlyne Patten Jordan; myself; my sister Bennie Jordan Creswell; my sister Rose Mary Jordan McGowan and her husband, John. *(Photo by Jerry Gibson, Houston Informer)*

At Harvard Commencement, 1977.
Gibson was a classmate at Boston U
versity. *(Photo by Rick Stafford, F
vard University News Office)*

Marian Anderson and I at the Harvard Commencement. *(Photo by Rick Stafford, Harvard University News Office)*

Texas Legislature yesterday in a Democratic primary that saw Texas liberals fail to take control of the state away from Governor John B. Connally, Jr. . . ."

In its next issue (May 20, 1966) *Time* magazine ran a full story accompanying a picture of Barbara and new Texas House member Curtis Graves, standing together beneath a sign that said VICTORY. Barbara was in her new yellow suit with black-and-white blouse; Graves, spectacled, was in conservative business suit and tie.

Headed TEXAS, A QUIET CHANGE, it read:

"Alabama's May 3 primaries proved that reasonably qualified white candidates can be elected in predominantly Negro counties. In Texas, where race is not an all-consuming political issue, the election results showed, in turn, that capable Negro office seekers can win the white support necessary for victory. In Houston the voters sent to the Texas Legislature its first two Negro members in 71 years: Attorney Barbara Jordan, 30, and Bank Executive Curtis M. Graves, 27.

"The Negro victories were facilitated by court-ordered reapportionment, under which the city was awarded ten additional legislative seats—several of them representing districts with large non-white populations. However, neither Democratic candidate campaigned exclusively on race, but concentrated instead on bread-and-butter issues that concern whites as much as Negroes in their working-class district . . .

"The result attested to a quiet change in the minds of many white Americans. Though 52% of the eligible voters in Miss Jordan's district are Negroes, she amassed 64.8% of the total vote—winning 30% to 50% of the ballots in white precincts and losing decisively in only one. Conducting a similarly restrained campaign for a House seat in a

47% Negro district, Banker Graves compiled 50.3% of the vote, polling 25% and 40% of the total non-Negro precincts. Since neither faces a Republican opponent in November, their primary victories—the first that Southern Negroes have yet won outright in this year's campaign for state offices—assure both candidates of election."

The law had allowed Barbara, at last, to enter the all-white world of the Good Old Boys.

6. AUSTIN

When Barbara drove her new Olds to Austin to begin her term in the Texas Senate, she found a place of familiar legends.

A clever cartoonist from the House poked the requisite fun, with the customary pride, at typical members of the legislature:

—A caption below an octogenarian on roller skates and a pretty weightlifter in spangled tights, read: "It's not difficult to tell who the single members are."

—A big, hairy-chested cowboy in ten-gallon hat, hands on his guns, declared: "The people want law and order, let's give them LAW AND ORDER."

—An affluent solon in patent-leather shoes, three-piece suit, slicked-down hair, taking his ease in a private club, lifted his martini to toast: "Drink wet, vote dry."

It was a world where the least politically astute bystander had heard tales of the annual party where the senators left their wives at home and brought their girlfriends.

Legislation at the Texas Capitol dealt with the same old

things: the volume of proposed bills on the state's most essential asset, water (pollution, depletion, subsidence), ran second only to bills to bolster the state's most lagging asset, education.

Lots of talk and lots of hours went into the typical frontier battles over liquor, guns, and law enforcement. In Barbara's first term, the Sixtieth Legislature, a five-cent tax per serving was imposed on alcoholic beverages in private clubs, but an attempt to vote in the governor's proposal to authorize the sale of whiskey for public on-premise consumption was defeated. The same session amended the penal code to raise the penalty for carrying weapons wherever beer or wine was sold or consumed to a felony, with punishment of five years in the penitentiary.

The Legislature convened the second Tuesday in January of every odd year. At a salary of $400 a month plus limited per diem and travel expenses, the usual senator did not come to Austin for financial gain. He came for that deceptive ambience of power which state houses glaze over their members. All-male, all-white, predominantly conservative, nine-tenths Democrat, two-thirds lawyers—with the rest usually in ranching, if from West Texas, or lumber, if from East Texas—the lawmakers did their best to limit membership in the club to others of the same ilk. It looked as if they had managed: The redistricting mandate that had made possible Barbara's victory had allowed one of the incumbents to gerrymander out the sole woman then in the Senate, Neville Colson of Navasota.

Barbara arrived, an exception to every rule. To reporters who ganged around to see how this black female from Fifth Ward in Houston was fitting into this closed world, she answered tartly: "As it turned out, the Capitol stayed on its foundations and the star didn't fall off the top."

It stayed in place, and the Senate gradually relaxed, because Barbara remained an exception. She made it clear there would be no need to rewrite the rules.

She took her own advice (delivered to the Lincoln, Nebraska, NAACP in a speech): "Throw away your crutches and quit complaining because you are black. Don't belch, choke, smoke, and wish for something to go away. Because when you are finished belching, choking, smoking, and wishing, society will still be here."

Her still-increasing bulk worked for her. She was massive, commanding, safe. She didn't look like their dear old mother, and she didn't look like their beauteous young girlfriend, so none of the old patterns needed to operate. Here was someone cut from a different mold, who, being outside their standard frame of reference, would not disrupt it.

Moving slowly, on schedule, Barbara hired a young woman with years of Capitol experience to run her office, Marlee Baker; and another, Nita Silberstein, to handle the secretarial work.

She studied the committee structure, so that when she met with the presiding officer of the Senate, Lieutenant Governor Preston Smith, she would know what to ask for. She requested State Affairs, as that was an important committee, and Labor and Management Relations, because of her strong labor backing. Smith, who had also done his homework and intended to get what mileage he could from acknowledging her, made her vice chairman of Labor Relations, put her on State Affairs, and named her to nine other committees in addition.

Next, she called upon the dean of the Senate, A. M. Aiken, feeling that she could start with him out of a deep, long-term respect. "Growing up, all I heard from my

Grandmother Gar was that her salary increases were due to the Gilmer-Aiken bill, that the small size of her classroom was due to the Gilmer-Aiken bill. I thought this man who co-authored the bill which structured public-school financing had done everything that had ever been done for education. To me, at that point, he represented the government of the State of Texas."

She put the senators at their ease at the earliest social gatherings. "I wanted them to see me firsthand and not just read about this great thing that had happened in Houston. I wanted them to know I was coming to be a senator, and I wasn't coming to lead any charge. I was not coming carrying the flag and singing 'We Shall Overcome.' I was coming to work and I wanted to get that message communicated personally.

"I recall at one of our first receptions, a group of senators was talking, and as I walked up one was saying: 'And you know that no good son-of-a-bitch.' And by this time he had noticed that I was there, and he said, 'Barbara, I am so sorry, I am so sorry.' I said: 'If a person is a no good son-of-a-bitch, then he's a no good son-of-a-bitch.' So he said, 'Well, okay,' and went right on with his story. And I didn't try to use salty language because that would make me one of them, but I just wanted them to be comfortable, and not to keep saying: 'Excuse me,' 'Pardon me.' "

So well did this work that she was invited to bring her guitar along and join Senator Charles Wilson's annual quail hunt, hitherto an all-male junket.

As expected, she allied herself with the liberal senators, a group of eleven led by Babe Schwartz of Galveston. But, surprisingly, she took most of her cues from the conservatives. Chief mentor was Dorsey Hardeman, the best of breed of the old school: believing that what the public didn't know wouldn't hurt it; adept at slipping controversial clauses into routine bills; insistent upon getting into the records his flourishing recognition of such matters as Nebraska's centennial statehood, the hundredth anniversary of Alaska's acquisition from Russia, Mississippi's sesquicentennial, and Canada's Centenary Confederation.

"I decided that Dorsey Hardeman from San Angelo knew the rules better than anybody. I think he wrote most of them, and I had seen him make a fool out of people just by pulling a rule on them. So I had to become acquainted well with Dorsey. In order to gain his respect, I, too, had to know the rules. One day I sought to pass a pollution control bill by obfuscating some parliamentary fine points —a tactic for which Hardeman was noted and which he practiced masterfully. I almost succeeded until Senator Hardeman started to listen to what I was saying. He asked: 'What are you trying to do?' I said: 'I'm using the tricker's tricks.'

"I used to talk to Dorsey a lot and I started dropping by his office for a drink in the afternoon. Now, that is really in, when you can do that. One of my friends at that time from Houston, Jake Johnson, who was in the House when I got to the Senate, came over looking for me one afternoon and couldn't find me, and somebody told him: 'Well, you can check in Senator Hardeman's office.' And when Jake walked in—Jake was a liberal House member, and Dorsey was the conservative leader of the Senate—and there I was, sitting on the couch with my feet on a chair and a drink in my hand, and Dorsey was sitting at his desk with a drink in his hand, Jake said he decided there was nothing he needed to worry about where I was concerned."

Hardeman, on his part, delighted in his role as teacher to

this unlikely neophyte. "I remember helping her one time to break up a filibuster. Barbara was handling a bill in the Senate, and you had to have a little co-operation from the lieutenant governor to do that, and Smith was a close friend of mine, so I made a motion to adjourn. When we went back in session I got recognized by prearrangement and wrote out a privileged motion for her to present. So we carried it; she learned how to get things off the floor."

A gracious, old-school gentleman, he conceded, "I was raised different. But she conducted herself in a most commendable manner from the start. Not forward in any respect. She didn't press her race or color. She was very modest and circumspect, which gained her the respect of the Senate.

"One time, I recall, Senator Bernal, a Mexican from San Antonio, was debating with Barbara, and he referred to a 'nigger-shooter' and they changed it to a 'Mexican-shooter,' and it was all in good fun. She got along from the start.

"We didn't vote alike," Hardeman concluded, "but hell, if that mattered, I'd be mad at half my friends."

■

One of the things I learned at Boston was that you can't work all the time. You can't maintain a public face all the time.

You need friends you can be with who don't care what your title is; who would never ask you to come and address the League of United Citizens of America, but who would come just because you're a person they want to be with.

I knew friends like the Justices were always going to be my friends; they would follow me anywhere and they did not ask for anything, because they were there in the beginning.

But out here in the white world it took a long time to decide the criteria for whom you could trust, and it was a judgment call every time. I would not be able to write down the rules for judging people, but it was just there in my head. Some people fit, and some people didn't, and you learned over the passage of time which ones would and which ones wouldn't.

Back when I had made speeches for everybody because I was trying to get myself well-known locally in Houston, I had spoken at the YWCA; and at one of those things you do at the Y on human relations, I had met Anne Appenzellar from Austin. And when I came to Austin to speak at such affairs as Girls' State, Anne would be the one to meet my plane.

So when I got to the Senate and got a place with two bedrooms and a bath on Norwalk Lane, and Anne lived nearby on Enfield Road, our acquaintance developed in a more casual way because I was now present on the scene.

And through Anne I met Betty Whitaker, who is a church-related person, not a Y person, and we would go visit Betty and eat seven-blade steaks, which was back to the old days for me.

On many occasions we would go to Betty's house. And one time Anne wanted to know if I would be interested in going to Inks Lake on a camping trip. Which I did do. And there was Betty and Anne and everybody, and we would camp out in tents and light fires and get dressed in the morning and sleep on air mattresses and all that sort of business. Sometimes we would fish and troll in the streams. And I thought: It's nice for me to be associated with all these people with these outdoorsy interests.

Sometimes we would pick up other people and go out to Betty's property on the lake, where she intended to put a trailer, and the other people would be clearing brush, Anne and Betty and Caroline Dowell, and I'd be sitting in the car, not even getting a look at the lake, but part of this camping troop . . .

When Betty got her trailer, which she had parked on a space that was not the lake, she said that we had to pick an evening for all our friends to come to christen the trailer. And I said: "Fine." So one night after I finished up my work in the Senate, Anne picked me up and took me to Betty's trailer.

At some point in the evening Nancy Earl arrived, and that was the first time we'd met face to face. From time to time, Betty and Anne would talk about this fine person, Nancy Earl, who worked at the University of Texas, and I did not know who they were talking about. It seemed Nancy got to be Anne's friend when she used to park her car at the Y and would come in to pay her five dollars each month.

Nancy and I sat there playing the guitar; we had just met but we were singing and drinking and having a swell time. All of us were, although Anne wasn't a real drinker, and Betty wasn't either. Then when it was time to turn out the lights of the campground where Betty's trailer was, Nancy invited us over: "Well, come to my place and we'll finish."

We all left and I was riding back with Anne and we were heading for Nancy's, when Anne got an attack of hay fever or something. So we didn't go to Nancy's. But I had had a great time and enjoyed myself very much. I remember I thought: This is something I would like to repeat. I'd like to have another party like that. Nancy Earl is a fun person to be with.

We all did have other parties. There were many other occasions where I could relax and enjoy myself.

At some point we had a big party at Nancy's and had Bennie and Rose Mary. Something was going on—I was being sworn in or *sine die*-ing—it was always the start of the session or the end of the session. We went out to the Trading Post and then we went back and partied until some wee hour of the morning.

I liked to be part of those parties. I had discovered I could relax at parties like that where I was safe.

■

While Barbara was consolidating these public and private alliances, the folks back home chafed because they had put her in office and had heard nothing from her. Where were the FIRST WOMAN, FIRST BLACK headlines they had come to expect? Whatever happened to Barbara Jordan?

What happened was that she bided her time. "You don't get in there having a drink quickly. You work and you learn the rules and you keep your mouth shut until it is time to open it."

The first time she spoke out in a way to receive the press's attention, was not on the floor of the state Senate, but around an oval table at the White House.

In February 1967, a month after she was sworn into office, Barbara received an invitation to confer with President Johnson on his proposed Fair Housing legislation. "I was just aghast at getting this kind of wire. It required a big summit meeting with everyone who had anything to do with me. I asked them: 'Should I just pick up and go to this meeting in Washington?' I said: 'It means I will have to miss a day at the Senate.' But they said: 'A telegram from the President of the United States is a summons, and certainly you must go.' I thought: Now, the meeting is at ten o'clock, so I probably don't need to stay overnight. I can just carry a tote bag and leave it in a locker in the terminal and pick it up that evening. Which I did. I flew into Dulles Airport and took the little bus into the Albert Pick Motor Inn, where I got a taxi, went to the White House, and presented my telegram at the gate."

Joining a collection of black civil rights leaders in the cabinet room—Roy Wilkins, Whitney Young, Dorothy Height—Barbara wondered if the President had any idea who she was, or if some aide had said to him: "Look, we ought to include that black woman who got elected down there in Texas."

The group rose as the President entered. He shook hands all around, touching and handling in his own personal style.

Housing, he told them, was the next offensive in integration. He intended to give it his full support. Then, as they filled their notepads, he went over the various points of his Fair Housing bill. "Now let's hear from some of you." He looked at his assemblage of faces. "Barbara, what do you think of this?"

Trying to sound calmer than she was, she made a brief statement, not sure what she had said or what impression she had made. "Well, Mr. President, this seems like a proper time to move on this legislation. It won't be easy. It will take work . . ."

After the meeting she took the taxi and the limousine, got her tote bag from the locker, and flew back to Austin.

The impact she had made, as well as the President's endorsement of her, got full coverage in the Washington *Post* (February 24, 1967) in Rowland Evans and Robert Novak's column headed LBJ GUESTS CHOSEN CAREFULLY, which read:

"When President Johnson summoned civil rights leaders to the White House, February 13, for a private preview of his 1967 civil rights message, the unpublished roster of those present showed startling omissions.

"The heads of two major civil rights groups—Stokeley Carmichael of the Student Non-violent Co-ordinating Committee (SNICK) and Floyd McKissick of the Congress of Racial Equality (CORE)—were not even invited. Nor was Bayard Rustin, who planned the march on Washington, or Joseph Rauh, civil rights spokesman for the Americans for Democratic Action (ADA). Dr. Martin Luther King of the Southern Christian Leadership Conference (SCLC) was invited, but didn't come.

"What's more, there were unfamiliar faces present—for instance, Texas State Senator Barbara Jordan. A Houston lawyer who is the only Negro in the Texas Senate, Miss Jordan lacks the national notoriety of Stokeley Carmichael and Floyd McKissick. But also unlike them, she is a practical politician who understands reality.

"The omissions and inclusions on that invitation list reveal how far President Johnson's sophistication in the politics of civil rights has progressed in the last two years.

". . . Had President Johnson not scheduled for the Feb.

13 briefing at the last moment, many Negro state legisla-
tors besides Miss Jordan would have been present. As it is,
the White House was far more impressed with her than
the usual run of civil rights leaders."

The next month, Barbara spoke up again, this time on
the floor of the Senate. Her maiden speech was a well-
thought-out event. "Rather than make a speech about oppression daily, I singled out one issue. I felt people in a
very bottom way were fair, and I felt I could appeal to this
fairness and reasonableness in my colleagues when the right
matter came along."

The thrust of her first speech, in support of liberal leader
Babe Schwartz's opposition to adding a 1 per cent city sales
tax to the existing state sales tax, was a question:

"Texas is number one in poor people because of its
regressive tax structure. The poor people of this state pay
approximately thirty per cent of their income in taxes.
Where is the equity when the people who make the most
pay the least, and the people who make the least pay the
most?"

Schwartz, pleased that she spoke out for him, responded
with a gallant speech praising her maiden effort, and there
was a round of applause that "their Barbara" had had her
say.

By the time she presented her first bill, she had learned
to take advantage of this mutual trust. "I am a member of
two groups long discriminated against in Texas politics.
But I discovered that the weight of those factors, that are a
part of whatever I am, will sometimes cause people to vote
for an issue I am in favor of rather than against it."

Being black and female helped in the passage of her Fair
Employment Practices Act, which came out of the Labor
and Management Relations Committee to pass the Senate

30 to 1. As one conservative explained his support: "I couldn't vote against it with a Negro lady for it."

Senate Bill 79 created the Fair Employment Practices Commission and provided for the regulation of discriminatory acts in employment. It declared it to be unlawful for a labor organization to "discriminate against any individual or to limit, segregate, or classify its membership in any way that would tend to deprive the individual of employment opportunities, limit his employment opportunities or otherwise affect adversely his status as an employee or as an applicant for employment, or that would affect adversely his wages, hours, or conditions of employment, on account of race, color, religion, national origin, sex, or age of the individual."

Barbara noted realistically that another reason her bill passed so easily was that it had "gums but no teeth." There was no effective avenue for guaranteeing its provisions. As she pointed out, "There was no civil rights or human relations committee in Texas that a plaintiff could appeal to, and the idea of withholding state funds to enforce equal hiring was a pipedream at that time."

She had served her apprenticeship through such steps as supporting Schwartz's bill and enacting a watered-down bill of her own; by the end of the session, she had learned the rules well enough to buck both the conservative faction over a voter registration plan, and the liberal clique over a spending bill proposal by the governor.

This latter involved a budget fight between Connally and Lieutenant Governor Preston Smith, with the governor claiming that his plan was more liberal, as it had certain education measures that the Senate's Finance Committee plan did not. The specific issue hinged on whether there would be enough votes to suspend the rules to take up the

Finance Committee's budget—and every liberal's vote was needed to block it.

But Barbara's loyalty was to Smith rather than Connally. "This little band of eleven—me, Schwartz, Mauzy, Brooks —were expected to back him. But I didn't feel I owed him anything. There had never been any occasion when Governor Connally had sent for Senator Barbara Jordan for any purpose. When I went to the White House I asked myself: 'I wonder what John Connally thought of that?' And I answered: 'He didn't think much.' Besides, I remembered when he opposed the Public Accommodations Act. It was not necessary for state legislatures to implement the federal act; the governor had only to encourage the people to go ahead and comply with the law. If the governor of the state said: 'This is the law and let's not fight it,' that was all it took. But to have the governor say: 'This is a bad idea and I'm opposed to it.' Well, it was a real turndown. So I didn't feel I owed John Connally anything."

When word reached the press that Jordan was the one Senate holdout in blocking the lieutenant governor's budget, the San Angelo *Standard Times* (May 14, 1967), headlined: NEGRO WOMAN SENATOR MAY HOLD KEY:

"It could be that when the showdown comes and if it does come, between Governor John Connally and Lt. Governor Preston Smith on the state spending bill, the freshman senator from Houston, Barbara Jordan, the senate's only woman and only Negro, will have the deciding vote.

". . . Both sides have been meeting with senators, and the latest score card indicates that the outcome will be very close. It could easily go to a 16–15 roll call, and one who remains firm on refusing to make a commitment is Senator Jordan.

"A lawyer, 31, Miss Jordan has operated quietly from a front corner desk in the Senate since she took office in January.

"But last week, she declared war, for the first time, on a voter registration bill by Senator Tom Creighton of Mineral Wells.

". . . If it turns out that hers is the swing vote, it could be that her decision will be influenced at least to some extent on which side will help her change the voter registration law.

". . . Senator Jordan, a senator because of the one man, one vote rule which broke big Harris County into four and a fraction senatorial districts, is well-respected in the Senate.

"It could turn out that her decision will be the Senate's on this big issue."

"Hear you got the key," Dorsey Hardeman hailed her the next day. "Hold on to it. Nobody else I'd trust more than you with the key."

Barbara went to the Speaker of the House, Ben Barnes, to say that she could not support Connally, and that she would help to get Smith's Senate budget bill worked out in conference committee in a way that would satisfy the House as well.

This was done and Barbara had the future support of both Smith and Barnes. She had as well the knowledge that she could get things done behind the scenes in the Texas Senate, that she knew the rules that were not in the book and how to apply them.

She and the Senate club had come a long way in her first
term. Far enough that she could say to her colleagues when
they elected her Outstanding Freshman Senator: "When I
first got here we approached one another with suspicion,
fear, and apprehension. But now I can call each one of you
singularly *friend*." And they could feel safe, and good, to
hear that.

In 1966, because of redistricting, each of the state senators had had to run for re-election, and in order to retain
staggered terms, had drawn for two-year or four-year
slots. Barbara had got a two-year term; in 1968, when she
ran again, she was re-elected for a four-year term.

Things had moved along by then. For one thing, John
Connally, scenting a future in national politics, had left the
governorship. Which was just as well in Barbara's mind, as,
by that summer, her feelings for him had hardened even
further.

She had stood on the platform with him at HemisFair in
San Antonio when word reached the crowd of Martin
Luther King's death. She recalled with grief his unfeeling
statement that "Those who live by the sword die by the
sword." She couldn't forget that, and in midsummer, at the
Democratic Convention in Chicago, when she learned of
the favorite-son movement for Connally, she flared up:
"Why, that son-of-a-bitch. How does he think he can be
anyone's favorite anything?"

Things were friendlier at the capital. Preston Smith had
moved into the vacated governor's spot; and House
Speaker Ben Barnes had been elected to the fiscally con-
trolling lieutenant governor's job. So now, with a governor
who was her friend and ally, Barbara made many trips to
his office and had many conferences with him on pending

matters. She spent afternoons with Barnes in his capitol apartment, plotting strategy over drinks with him and lobbyist friend Frank Erwin.

The national Democratic Party had discovered her and she and Barnes were part of a planeload of Texans flown by Bob Strauss to Miami for a fund-raiser—to which Barbara wore a new gold dress, gold shoes which hurt her feet, her mother's fur stole, and her first pair of pantyhose—to hear Sammy Davis, Jr., perform, and to pose for pictures with Ted Kennedy.

She was given all she could handle in Senate assignments. Barnes appointed her chairman of the Labor and Management Relations Committee; vice chairman of the Legislative, Congressional, and Judicial committees; made her a member of Education, Environmental Matters, Finance, Interstate Co-operation, Jurisprudence, Nominations, Privileges and Elections, State Affairs, State Departments and Institutions, and Youth Affairs committees. In addition to these monumental committee assignments, she carried the workman's compensation reform package, and legislation on unemployment compensation.

The legislature even, at last, passed a liquor-by-the-drink law, which meant that for the first time since the state ratified the prohibition amendment, Texans could buy intoxicating beverages in public places.

But halfway through her second term, the day of Smith's and Barnes's second inauguration, on January 18, 1971, this honeymoon came to an end. A splashy exposé of rumored corruption, called the "Sharpstown Scandal," hit every newspaper in the state, bringing cries of reform with the primary election still fifteen months away.

Most implicated was thirty-eight-year-old Speaker of the House Gus Mutscher, a conservative Democrat, eventually fingerprinted and charged with a felony in a lawsuit, filed by the Federal Securities and Exchange Commission, which alleged that he and a number of prominent Texas businessmen had taken part in financial transactions which artificially manipulated the price of stock in the National Bankers Life Insurance Company, enabling them to buy low and sell at a falsely elevated high.

For Smith and Barnes, this put a damper on their claims of a clean house, and on their political futures. For Barbara, the scandal had only peripheral effect. Her main worry: that it might end the career of Barnes. "I was afraid it would hurt Ben. I considered that regrettable because I didn't believe he was involved. I had established a friendship with him and was always impressed with his political savvy and kept hoping he would not be tarnished by it. So that's how I spent my time over Sharpstown—just hoping that it would not hurt Ben."

As the scandal continued to unfold, Barbara took care not to take sides in the growing friction between Barnes and Smith. She was loyal to both of them, and did not want to be caught in the middle when Barnes opposed Smith for governor.

Meanwhile, less newsworthy but closer to home, she got involved in accusations that she had sold out the Eleventh Senatorial District to get herself a seat in the U. S. Congress.

The 1970 census had reorganized existing congressional seats on the basis of the one person, one vote rule. Texas ended up, due to increased state population, with one additional seat. And this in Houston.

Barbara decided that if the new congressional district were favorable to her, she would run for it while she had the chance, before she had an incumbent to face. Barnes promised that he would do what he could to help; which he did by naming her vice chairman of the Redistricting Committee. And everything went as planned. "Bob Eckhardt could feel me breathing down his neck in Houston, and he wanted something to work out so that I could go to Congress without his having to come home. So we drew these districts and everybody was safe. At one point Schwartz, who wanted to come to Congress at that time, came in at midnight with a plan of his own that included a big chunk of his hometown Galveston running into Houston, but when he left we got back to our maps and pencils, setting the boundaries as agreed."

With the new congressional seats taken care of and not wanting to get involved in the hassle of rearranging senatorial slots, the Senate turned over the job of redistricting the upper state house to the Legislative Redistricting Board: composed of the Lieutenant Governor, the Speaker of the House, the Attorney General, the Land Commissioner, and the Comptroller.

Bitterness followed when it appeared that the old Eleventh Senatorial District had been sacrificed for the new congressional spot. House member Curtis Graves, who had been elected to the Texas lower house when Barbara was elected to the Senate, had assumed he would move up into her place when she moved on. He was outraged. "She has sold us out," he screamed.

Barbara realized that the Senate had already determined that her old district would be carved up in such a way that Graves could not get elected, but decided there was nothing she could do about it.

Eckhardt put the blame on the Good Old Boys. "I was

in Ben Barnes's office when he said the Senate was determined not to let Graves in. It was not Barbara's trade-off.
Graves was rather flamboyant and they didn't want him."

Graves brought a suit to federal court seeking to void
the Harris County plan as enacted in October by the Legislative Redistricting Board, charging that the five members
had drawn Senate district lines that prevented any black
from Houston from ever going again to the state Senate.

Claiming that the maps were drawn with the intention
of "systematically disenfranchising blacks and depriving
them of the right to elect a senator responsive to their concerns," Graves ended with a threat: "If there is not a black
viewpoint in the Senate, you are going to have problems. If
people can't get their viewpoint presented in a legitimate
manner, then you run the danger that they will take illegit-
imate means to do so."

Barnes, called to the stands, denied intent. "There was
never anything done intentionally to dilute or minimize the
votes of any minority, especially the blacks."

Barbara, in a deposition, admitted that damage had been
done; that she doubted that a black could get elected from
the redrawn Eleventh District.

The Supreme Court, however, ruled that shifting the
Eleventh Senatorial District did not dilute black voting
strength in Harris County. With no chance now at the
Senate, Graves declared against Barbara for Congress.
Making his pitch for endorsement before the Harris
County Democrats, he claimed that his opponent had sold
out, that she was in the enemy camp, had been in cahoots
with the conservative mayor of Houston, Louie Welch,
and, a final betrayal, had refused to endorse the liberal candidate for governor, Sissy Farenthold, against Preston
Smith or Ben Barnes.

The Harris County Democrats had been through all this before. They knew their sympathies were with many of Graves's claims; they also knew he had the chances of a lame pony running in the Kentucky Derby. After the usual rancorous debate, they finally conferred a joint endorsement, and washed their hands.

At the end of October 1971, in downtown Houston, Barbara put on a gala fund-raising event to pay her way to Congress. Out came a new metallic gold-and-brown gown. Out came blacks and whites in black tie and white fur, to mingle with bankers and stockholders in the grand ballroom of the Rice Hotel. Her sisters, the Justices, their husbands, all the old friends were there, everyone except Ben Jordan—ill with heart trouble that had forced him to quit his job at the Houston Terminal Warehouse and Cold Storage—who was not able to join his youngest daughter for her party.

Jake Johnson, acting as financial adviser, called in all his cards to see that people with money came. And Barbara called in her trump, former President Lyndon B. Johnson, who had given her her most valuable political lesson: "Don't go for it unless it's already in your pocket."

"I'll tell you what prompted me to invite Lyndon Johnson to this fund-raiser. He came to Houston one time to speak, he was not President then, at a fund-raising affair for Ralph Yarborough. We were always paying off Ralph's campaign expenses, and we were raising money this time for paying off some of his debts, and Johnson was to speak for the occasion. And there was much discussion and debate as to who would introduce Lyndon Johnson. And it just never got settled because too many people wanted to do it. Well, Lyndon sent word to the committee that he wanted me to introduce him. That settled the matter for all time. So I introduced him well, and at the conclusion of this whole program Johnson took my hand—he had a way of holding both your hands, and he just looked you in the eye—and he said: 'Barbara, I've never been so introduced. I'm going to help you in whatever way I can help you get wherever you want to be. Anything. You just tell me what you need.' And I said: 'Thank you, I'll do that.'

"So I thought I would ask him to come to my fund-raising cocktail party. I sent him a letter to the ranch, and I didn't hear anything, but I felt that the fact that I didn't hear anything was a good sign.

"We proceeded to plan as if he would be there, and as the day approached, his secretary called to say: 'The President will be there. He will just arrive, don't pick him up; don't have an escort committee, he'll be there.' "

The night of the party, with her hair fixed by Wilma and an orchid on her shoulder, Barbara stood there hugging and kissing all the old friends from the Fifth Ward and all the new political friends from Austin and Houston, when a wild stir went up in the crowd.

Johnson had arrived.

The New York *Times* carried a picture of their embrace: her beaming face buried against his shoulder, him grinning widely as he clasped her in his big arms.

They worked the crowd together in Johnson style— touching, patting, shaking hands, pressing the flesh of all they could reach—to the podium, where the other speakers waited.

(There had been a big flap among Barbara's supporters when conservative Louie Welch had asked to be a part of the program; he was considered no friend to blacks. But

Barbara had waved that away: "If the mayor of the city of Houston wants to say a few words, he has to do that.")

Johnson fanned the cheering crowd of fifteen hundred with reminders of his dedication to civil rights, recounting to them a tale they loved about his black aide whose job it was to drive the Johnson car, clothes, diapers, and beagle home to Texas from Washington, while the family flew with the little girls. And about how the aide had protested taking Little Beagle Johnson, saying: "A nigger has enough hell getting through the South without taking a dog with him." Moved by this glimpse into the discrimination against blacks, he told them, he had determined to use every power he had to see that nobody would ever again have trouble finding a bathroom or a place to eat. "Or driving my dog from Washington to Texas."

Turning to the radiant candidate on the platform, he told them whom they had come to honor. "Barbara Jordan proved to us that black is beautiful before we knew what that meant," he said. "She is a woman of keen intellect and unusual legislative ability, a symbol proving that We Can Overcome. Wherever she goes she is going to be at the top. Wherever she goes all of us are going to be behind her." Then, bringing his two themes together with a flourish, he said: "Those with hurting consciences because they have discriminated against blacks and women can vote for Barbara Jordan and feel good."

He presented her with a copy of his just-published memoir of his years in the presidency, *Vantage Point*. He vowed that he gave the first copy to Lady Bird, the second to Bess Truman, the next ones to his daughters, and that now this copy was for Barbara. Making the crowd laugh by pointing out that if they wanted one of their own, they would be in the bookstores next week.

Barbara choked up when she rose to reply. "Mr. President, you make us all feel like first-class Americans," she said. "And we all enjoy feeling that way. I don't want anyone saying that Lyndon Johnson is not still the President of the United States. You will always be my President."

October 26, 1971

Dear Barbara,

You will note from attached that we made the NYT together. I'm delighted that I was able to share the reception with you and pay tribute to one of the most capable, caring ladies I know.

Your deeply touching and generous letter added to my warm memories of a wonderful evening. I'm so grateful for all you said.

LBJ

The state began the spring of 1972 on a familiar note: oil. Taking account of the energy shortage now beginning to be felt by the voters, the Railroad Commission responded to the demand for crude oil by ordering maximum production from the Texas fields starting in March.

The legislature, not in regular session in even years, had one last order of business to tend to: saying goodbye to Barbara. Secure in the knowledge that the Eleventh Senatorial District as newly constituted guaranteed the election of longtime regular Chet Brooks, and that their favorite anomaly was safely on her way out of Texas to Washington, they could give her one last salute. They resolved to make her Governor for a Day.

Traditionally, the president pro tem of the Senate, the third in command, becomes governor in the absence from the state of the governor and lieutenant governor. In fact, it has become an automatic affair, paid for by the lobbyists, that each pro tem have his day, for the delight of his constituents, at an agreed-upon time when the higher officials make token disappearances.

Lieutenant Governor Barnes called a quick session in March to deal with billboards on the highways, and Barbara was named president pro tem. The date for her ceremony was set for June tenth—by which time Smith and Barnes would each be through with the primary and would have been elected or defeated.

This business taken care of, the members of the Senate club could heave a sigh of relief and go back to where they had been before: closing ranks to all but white male colleagues like themselves.

Senator A. M. Aiken: "We don't think of her as a member of any race. We think of her as a great Texan and a great American."

Leon Jaworski: "Governor Jordan stands before you as the central figure in a new page in Texas history."

Bill Hobby: "She does us honor by redeeming this state. She will be my very own congressman."

Houston *Chronicle*, June 11, 1972. Dateline Austin: "State Senator Barbara Jordan, a poor black girl from Houston's poverty-bound Fifth Ward, made her way into the history books Saturday . . ."

My dear friends,

"Governor for a Day" celebrations are traditional and old. This day is open and new for me. It is time to focus on the past and renew my search for meaning in the future.

The past holds as its prisoner indifferent interpersonal relationships, pain and poverty, fears and frustrations. The past reminds us of dreams deferred and killed; of growth stunted as we struggled to touch and feel a man's humanity.

What about the future? What are its offerings? The future can mean a Bold New Venture for Texas. It can mean an end to poverty and human suffering. The future can signal the beginning of a New Commitment by the Government of the State of Texas to the People of the State of Texas. This must be a commitment which recognizes that the quality of a man's life is measured by his job, health, home, school, environment, spirit, and opportunity for personal growth and development. My faith in this State and its people makes me optimistic that this commitment will be made and fulfilled.

I extend my eternal gratitude to my Senate colleagues and the citizens of the Eleventh Senatorial District for giving me this day.

Barbara Jordan

PROCLAMATION by the Governor of the State of Texas
ALL TO WHOM THESE PRESENTS SHALL COME:
WHEREAS, The 11th Senatorial District plays a vital and commanding role in medical research of disease control through both public and private hospitals and research facilities and the many famous and distinguished physicians, surgeons, and scientists who staff them; and

WHEREAS, A national health problem, and one that is proportionally great in Texas, is the purge of sickle cell, which has blighted our shores ever since the first slaves were landed in Virginia in 1619, though the disease remained unidentified in America until 1910; and

WHEREAS, This blood disease is inherited and is found principally in Black People; in mild form, known as sickle cell trait, it is found in one out of ten Black Americans, or approximately two million, while its severe form, known as sickle cell anemia, is evidenced in at least 50,000 persons in the United States, and

WHEREAS, The changes of genetic transmission of the trait and the disease are high, although the disease is not infectious and many persons are unaware of carrying the sickle cell gene; patients with sickle cell anemia experience severe pain and suffering as well as low resistance to infections, and life span is considerably reduced with an estimated 50 per cent of sickle cell disease sufferers dying before the age of 20 and the remainder rarely living beyond middle age; and

WHEREAS, No cure has yet been discovered for sickle cell anemia largely because the disease has been a veritable stepchild of medical research; however, a national spotlight, to bring some light to the sad plight of far too many Black youngsters, has finally been turned on with an appropriation by the Congress of $114 million over a three-year period, during which public education, medical research, genetic counseling, and health care will be intensified; thus, there is now promise for all afflicted Black citizens, including the estimated 106,700 Texans carrying the sickle cell trait and the 2,700 with sickle cell anemia, and

WHEREAS, The Sickle Cell Disease Research Foundation of Texas, Incorporated, has been created and located in Houston with the objective to "inform the general public and to sponsor programs for detection, diagnosis, treatment and research in the field of sickle cell and related blood diseases"; Baylor College of Medicine and Texas

Children's Hospital have joined the Foundation in the pursuit of these objectives;

NOW, THEREFORE, I, BARBARA JORDAN, GOVERNOR OF TEXAS, in recognition of the indicated and important work of the Sickle Cell Disease Research Foundation of Texas, Incorporated, and its affiliated hospitals and medical schools, do hereby salute the efforts of these dedicated citizens of Texas who are selflessly concerned about their fellow man and who have taken determined steps to implement this concern; in token of this recognition I do hereby proclaim the Month of September A.D. 1972 as SICKLE CELL DISEASE CONTROL MONTH IN TEXAS, urging that each citizen support the work of the Sickle Cell Disease Research Foundation of Texas, Incorporated, and its affiliates to the end that the State of Texas will be identified as a state that cares for all its people.

When I came up for that special session, I knew that the first order of business would be the election of a president pro tem. And I knew that I would be that president pro tem for that special session. As a matter of fact, I wore a dark-blue dress that would look all right on television that morning.

First came the nomination, and then we voted, and the vote is always thirty people aye, one present, because you don't vote for yourself. Then I made a brief little acceptance speech, and I knew I was going to have a Governor for a Day ceremony. Even though at the conclusion of that special session they would elect another pro tem for the interim, that did not prevent my ceremony.

Then I worked with Ben and Preston to set up a time when they would both be ostensibly out of the state, and we settled on June 10, 1972. That is because by that date the primary election would be over, and I would have already won the Democratic nomination to the Congress, and each of them would have won or lost his bid for governor, and I had not endorsed either of them.

Then I got my silver tray. Each pro tem got a huge silver tray which had a seating chart of the Senate etched on one side, and the signatures of all the senators on the other. Each member of the senate contributed ten dollars to the tray of each pro tem.

Next, my secretary, Nita, and I arranged the program. I had decided that I wanted to make it possible for all of the high schools in the old Eleventh Senatorial District to come. I said to Nita: "We're going to invite each one of them, and anybody who cannot pay to come, we will offer to pay for them." Well, the buses came carrying the high schools, the junior high schools, the TSU choir which was to be on the program to sing, the entire Fifth Ward. I am told that there was no business on Lyons Avenue open that June tenth, 1972. I am told that everyone was in Austin for that Governor for a Day.

The first event of the day was a breakfast that morning at the governor's mansion for me and my family, which everybody attended except my father. He was still sick with his heart problem, but he had said that it would be okay, that he wanted to go to Austin because he was definitely not going to miss that day of mine. He had been driven up in a big Cadillac that he inherited from his uncle, and had a new white jacket and a carnation and all. But during that breakfast he was resting, saving himself for the big occasion.

The second event was that main ceremony in the Senate chamber. The senators were seated in their seats, and the speakers were up on the platform, but everybody else was in the gallery. Well, I thought that the gallery had been blacked out on the day I was sworn in the Senate, but on this June tenth you could not even squeeze a gnat through the door. And they could yell and they could applaud to their hearts' content. I did not have to tell them to be quiet, because I was the governor, and I could run my day the way I wanted to. So they yelled at everything.

I had decided that I wanted my speaker to be Leon Jaworski, who at that time was president of the American Bar Association. I though that would be appropriate. So I invited Jaworski to do the speech that day, which he consented to do of course. And Andrew Jefferson, my old friend from TSU who was then a Domestic Relations Court Judge in Houston, swore me in. I had A. M. Aiken, the dean of the Senate, introduce me as governor, and he drove all night from Paris, Texas, to be there. He said: "I came because Barbara said she wanted me to do this." And it was that sort of event.

I had a military escort and attendant and all that. The Confederate flag had been removed and I was accused of doing it, but I didn't. Someone else had removed it. And I had the minister from the Good Hope Missionary Baptist Church say the invocation. And on the platform there was my father, and my mother, and the other participants in the program.

Then the choir sang, and everyone spoke, and I gave my response. I really don't recall what I said, because it wasn't anything I worked on. I knew some of my colleagues would have used that occasion to give their state of the

State address, but I wanted it as a celebration for all of my friends, and that's just what it was.

The third event was a reception in the governor's office of the capitol, and you sat at the governor's desk and you signed proclamations, and then you stood in line and got gifts from various people who wanted to give them to you.

So while I was in the reception room of the governor's office Rose Mary kept trying to interrupt the line of people to say something to me, and when she finally broke through, she said: "Daddy got sick. There is nothing to worry about, but we've taken him to the hospital. Mother has gone with him."

So I went on shaking hands and greeting folks and receiving their good wishes, and at the conclusion of the reception I went down to my office and asked if there was any word from the doctor concerning how things were with my father.

I had given all of my Austin friends a specific assignment for this day, and one assignment that I gave to Anne Appenzellar was to get the name and telephone number of a doctor who would be available, because we knew my father was ailing and we wanted to be able to reach someone quickly. So Anne had all of the information in case a doctor was needed. She came to the office and told me that there had been a state police officer nearby with a walkie-talkie who got an ambulance for my father. I said: "How is he now?" She said: "Well, I don't know. Do you want me to go over there?" And I said that I did, that I wanted her to find out how things were.

Then there was a discussion with Nancy and these other people, that many folks knew that my father had been stricken but that most did not. We discussed if I should announce this news in the afternoon program. And I said: "No, I'm not going to do that. This is a day that people are supposed to be happy, and if I announce that, then that's all anybody will remember about the afternoon event. So there will be no mention of my father."

Having settled that, we went outside for lunch, which was a barbeque on the capitol grounds. The capitol hill guards said they had never seen anything like it. People would eat and then they would bundle up their paper and find a wastebasket and throw it in. We didn't have any maintenance problems because everybody was doing what they were supposed to do that day and everybody was just loving each other. The TSU choir sang, and the Phillis Wheatley Band and the Jack Yates Band played, and the young kids were doing the bugaloo on the capitol steps and there were some more speeches, and everybody was just having fun and getting pretty exhausted, as this was an all-day affair—when Anne reported back to me that it was a stroke that my father had had.

So I decided that before the evening affair I would go to the hospital. At that point I had the governor's black limousine and a driver and all that, so I went to Brackenridge Hospital to see my father.

I walked into the room and there he was on the bed with all of his teeth showing. Just the most wonderful smile imaginable. He didn't say much, because at that point his speech was somewhat impaired, but he had that wonderful expression on his face. I said: "Chief, you almost made the day." I said: "But you got to see me be governor." And he was still grinning. I said: "You just take care and don't worry. Everything's going to be fine."

Then I left and went back to my suite at the hotel.

That night we had scheduled a party, with Rose Mary and Bennie and the Justices and their husbands, and about two hundred and fifty other select friends, to hear Novella Nelson, whom I thought was one of the best singers I had ever heard. She and her bass player and piano player performed, and it was a fine evening of entertainment.

Then, at the conclusion of her singing, a strange lady came up to me and said: "Barbara, you need to go to the hospital."

I said: "Look, don't play games. Why do I need to go to the hospital?"

She said: "Well, your father needs you."

"Is he worse?" I asked her.

"Yes, he's worse."

So, okay. I rounded up Bennie and Rose Mary and told them what was happening. I grabbed Nancy and said, "Look, I'm going to the hospital, but you take everybody on out to the restaurant and I'll try to join you." You see, I had planned another little party for after the other big party, and that small gathering also included the singer Novella Nelson. I said: "You take the group and I'll be in touch. Do everything you know I'd want done. Just have fun."

Then the family went to the hospital. My father seemed to be sinking into a coma and there was nothing any of us could do at that point. My mother was there and she had been there ever since he was brought in. I was trying to get her to go back to the hotel, but she didn't want to, of course.

Finally I went back without her and changed from my black-and-white long dress into some street clothes, and talked on the phone to Nancy who was out with the small groups of friends, and she said that everyone had eaten and everyone was happy and pretty much tired out. So I told her to meet me at the hotel with anybody who still wanted to hang on and that we would go out to her house and do a final wrap-up with the guitar. And that's what we did.

Then I went back to the hotel and checked in with the hospital. By then it was early morning, already daylight. My mother was still there, and Mamie and Wilmer were there with her, but Bennie and Rose Mary had come back to their rooms to get some sleep. I persuaded my mother that we had made it to the light of day and that she really should get some rest.

I talked her into coming back to the hotel, and someone drove her there. But as soon as she arrived, we got a call from the hospital that my father was dying, so she had to turn around and go right back. Before we left the hotel, Anne asked me: "Do you know the name of a funeral director?" I told her: "Get the name and telephone number of Jackson Funeral Home in Houston." Then we got in the car and went immediately to my father.

We all sat in a waiting room a few steps down the hall from where he was: Bennie and Creswell, Rose Mary and John, Mamie and Wilmer, myself, Mother. We sat there while Nancy and Anne were back at command head-quarters at the hotel taking care of some of the out-of-town people from New York, dealing with all of that. We sat there until the doctor came in and said: "He's gone. Would you like to see him?"

I said that we would, and took my mother back to the room where she started to cry. Rose Mary said: "Now you better pull yourself together." But I said: "No, you cry. You've lost your man." I told Rose Mary: "This is her man who's gone." And Mamie said: "Yes, he really was her man."

My mother, close to the bed, whispered: "Are you sure he's gone?" I said: "Yes, he's gone." So we stayed in there another couple of minutes or so and then I took my mother back to the sitting room, and called the Jackson Funeral Home to see if they would come to Austin to remove the body. I learned from the hospital office that you needed some special something to release the body from Travis County, so I called Nita, my secretary, and said: "Look, will you come here and deal with the rules and regulations for getting the body out of here?"

The papers got signed and the body was removed and we all went back to my suite to find that Nancy and Anne had got everybody off in airplanes.

And my mother was very quiet at that point. I told her that I would like to do my father's eulogy, and she and my family were horrified. I was informed that only a preacher could do a eulogy. So that was the end of that idea. Then my mother started to talk about the fact that all of the preachers were out of town until Wednesday or Thursday, at a conference, so we would have to wait until then for the funeral service.

At that point I knew that there was no way that we were going to stand around until Wednesday, until the preachers got back. And I said that. But of course Wednesday, and ten preachers, it was going to be—because my mother said so.

The next day I stayed over to get myself settled down. I told Nancy: "You know, if my father had had the option of choosing a time to die, he would have chosen that day." That's the way I was feeling, that he got a chance to see the ceremony. He didn't embarrass himself by dying in the middle of Governor for a Day, which would have been unbearable for him. He had his moment on the platform. He had that.

Then Ed Brooke sent me an item which was reported in the New York *Times:*

FATHER SEES DAUGHTER
SWORN IN, DIES NEXT DAY

"Austin, Texas. June 11. (UPI). The Rev. Benjamin M. Jordan, father of State Senator Barbara Jordan of Houston, died today in an Austin hospital of a stroke he suffered while watching his daughter sworn in as Governor for a Day in Texas. He was admitted to the hospital yesterday.

"Senator Jordan, president pro tem of the Texas Senate, was sworn in yesterday as Governor for a Day, an honor given each year to the person holding the Senate post. The Governor and Lieutenant Governor absent themselves from the state for the day. She became the first black woman governor of any state."

And my mother said: "Do you see this? He died at a time when everybody knew it. In New York they know that he died!"

OBSEQUIES
for
REV. BENJAMIN M. JORDAN
Died: Sunday, June 11, 1972

If my people, which are called by my name, shall humble themselves and pray, and seek my face, and turn from their wicked ways; then will I hear from heaven, and will forgive their sin, and will heal their land. II Chronicles 7:14.

Wednesday, June 14, 1972—1:00 P.M.
at
Good Hope Missionary Baptist Church

ACTIVE PALLBEARERS:
Members of Heights Lodge #280
HONORARY PALLBEARERS:
Baptist Ministers Association
Ministers Wives Association
Deacons and Trustees
FLOWER BEARERS:
Members of Delta Sigma Theta Sorority
The Houston Links, Inc.

". . . On June 18, 1931, Ben was married to Arlyne Patten and three children were born during this marriage: Rose Mary, Bennie Meredith, and Barbara. The parents of these three daughters had as the major focus of their lives the provision of an education for their girls which would equip them to function as useful and productive citizens. Bennie and Rose Mary teach music in the Houston public schools. Barbara is a lawyer and a politician.

". . . On Saturday, June 10, 1972, Rev. Jordan saw Senator Barbara Jordan sworn in as 'Governor for a Day'. He said, 'I wanted to see THIS DAY . . . that Black Girl.' "

THREE

WORLD

"The problem remains that we fail to define ourselves in terms of whole human beings, full human beings. We reduce the definition of our lives just a little bit because somewhere in the back of our minds is the thought that we are really not quite equal. So what are women going to do about it? How are we going to change all that? It is going to take long, hard, slow, tedious work. And we begin with our own self-concept. We begin to try to internalize how we really feel about ourselves, and proceed to actualize the thinking that we finally evolve from the look inward and the projection outward."

7. ENTRANCE

The program for Fellows is highly selective. The present program enlists a minimum of six individuals in each of the two academic terms. Selection is guided in part by attempts to develop a representative roster in terms of specialization and experience, geographical distribution, party affiliation, and the categories of women and minority groups. Fellowship appointments are awarded by invitation, on the Institute's initiative.

Institute of Politics, Harvard

Before the Congress convened in January of 1973, I spent a month at what we called the Harvard Head Start. It was held in December for a few new members of Congress at the John F. Kennedy Institute of Politics. They paid us to go, and their theory was that freshman members needed help in making the transition to Congress. That they needed to know something about the agencies, the structure of the bureaus, how to select a staff, to know generally what a member of Congress does.

The Institute was directed by Mark Talisman, who was an administrative assistant to a relatively senior member of Congress, Charles Vanik of Ohio; Mark was considered the best administrative assistant on Capitol Hill.

Part of our orientation consisted of deciding what requests we would make for committee assignments once we got to Washington. Mark told us—Alan Steelman, Yvonne Burke, Bill Cohen, and me—that it was important to decide on our committee assignments and make those requests early. I talked to him about what I would like, and we mentioned the Judiciary Committee. In the meantime, the Congressional Black Caucus had decided that they would ask me to request the Armed Services Committee. The Caucus members had taken it upon themselves to look after me because Andy Young and I were the first blacks elected to Congress from the South since Reconstruction. So they were doing this. Now, members of Congress get one major committee and one minor committee assignment, and Judiciary and Armed Services are both major committees, which meant that I would have to decide between them. Mark and I chatted about that, and I told him that I bet LBJ would help me on the matter. So he said: "Well, why don't you see if he will?"

Which I did. I addressed a letter to Johnson and told him I was thinking about the Judiciary and Armed Services committees. It was a specific request that he help, primarily that he talk to Omar Burleson from Anson, Texas, who was a member of the Ways and Means Committee, which was the committee that made the other committee assignments. Also, that he talk to Wilbur Mills, who was the chairman of that committee.

Shortly after that I got a call at the faculty club where I was staying at Harvard, at the Institute. It was Johnson.

He told me: "I got your letter and I've already acted on it. I talked to Omar. I talked to Wilbur. I had some trouble finding him because he was off fishing someplace in Arkansas, but I interrupted his fishing and told him he had to get on your committee assignment right away."

I said: "Well, thank you, Mr. President. Thank you for doing that." Then I started to discuss the assignment specifically. Had he asked Wilbur Mills to look out for me for Armed Services or for Judiciary? Johnson said: "You don't want to be on the Armed Services Committee. People will be cursing you from here to there, and the defense budget is always a sore spot and people don't want to spend the money. You don't want that. What you want is Judiciary. If you get the Judiciary Committee and one day someone beats hell out of you, you can be a judge."

So that made sense, and I thanked him.

One further order of business that Mark helped us with was the selection of a staff. One day I went to Washington from Cambridge because I had interviews scheduled in Charles Vanik's office with about a dozen prospects. These interviews went on all morning. One thing I knew for certain, that I wanted people with some Hill experience. I felt we didn't all need to get to the office and not know which way to the ladies' room. It did not make sense to bring anyone from my Houston office, as no one had any more experience than I had. So I talked with a number of people who knew the capitol scene, and I hired about five people. I hired Bud Myers, my assistant, at that time. My thinking was, if I had a black and a man, that would satisfy everyone. He had worked as administrative assistant to Andy Jacobs, and so was already knowledgeable.

Then we got our committee assignments, and I got the Judiciary Committee. I was told that when the Ways and

Means Committee reached the matter of the Judiciary Committee on the agenda, Wilbur Mills said: "Now, after Barbara Jordan, who shall we put on here?" And being the first person named, I got seniority over any other freshman, which was important.

There were so many members of Congress. And I was coming from a 31-member state senate into that 435-member House of Representatives. It became obvious to me that it was going to be difficult to make any impact on anybody with all of these people also trying to make an impact, in order to create the impression back home among their constituents that they were outstanding.

The first thing was, I would have to get in good with my colleagues from Texas. I would be the unique new kid on the block to them, and I wanted to work comfortably with them. For instance, I knew that women had never been allowed to attend the Texas Democratic Delegation luncheon that had been meeting at twelve-thirty on Wednesdays since the early tenure of Sam Rayburn, and I intended to change that. Which I did.

Then we were officially sworn in. Before that session, one of my fellow Texans said that all the Texas delegation would stand around me for the swearing-in. And another said: "Well, now, but that might take away from Barbara Jordan. People might not be able to tell which one she is." I laughed and told him: "I think they'll be able to figure that out."

When that was over, I gave some thought to where I should sit on the floor of the House of Representatives. My conclusion was: You can hear better on the center aisle, and you can catch the eye of the presiding officer better on the center aisle, as you are in his direct line of vision. So I decided that is where I would always sit, leaving one seat next to me on the aisle vacant, for those people who might want to stop and visit from time to time.

I was accused of not wanting to sit with the liberals and the Congressional Black Caucus people, who sat to the far left, but that place near center aisle seemed the most advantageous location to me.

The evening of the swearing-in, Bob Eckhardt gave a reception for me, because he was so glad that we were both up there. The Texans in Washington gave a reception. And the Texas Southern University ex-students gave a reception. So we were thoroughly received.

Then almost immediately we got word that Lyndon Johnson had died. He had had a heart attack at the ranch. I was very saddened. I gave a statement on the floor of the House and I said: "The death of Lyndon Johnson diminishes the lives of every American involved with mankind. The depth of his concern for people cannot be quantified—it was big and all-encompassing." I said: "Old men straightened their stooped backs because Lyndon Johnson lived; little children dared look forward to intellectual achievement because he lived; black Americans became excited about a future of opportunity, hope, justice, and dignity." I said: "Lyndon Johnson was my political mentor and my friend. I loved him and I shall miss him."

I meant all of that. And at the bottom of my grief was the feeling that I was sitting up there all alone on that center aisle. Other people were always talking about what they had done for me. But Lyndon Johnson wasn't like that. He just did it and he didn't take credit for it.

■

"My asking Barbara to be on the Judiciary Committee was quite a feather in her cap. It was against all odds, as she was a freshman member, and people vied for the position. But as she was a black, a woman, and a lawyer, and since I wanted to do whatever I could to enhance the committee, as I was coming new as chairman, I felt certain she would be a valuable addition.

"As we began to get into impeachment she was articulate, balanced, not extremist. She began to display the ability to be concise and precise, but not aggressive. She was one who sat and listened; she followed my lead. I looked upon her as a protégé."

Peter Rodino
Chairman, Judiciary Committee

It was 1974 and the press and the people were rumbling about Watergate. Talk was heavy. But I was discounting all that, thinking: "Nothing like that is going to happen. You're talking about the presidency. You're not going to impeach the President."

Well, resolutions were introduced, and pressure was being placed on the Speaker, and on the Judiciary Committee, and on Peter Rodino to do something. The pressure built up in the Congress and among the people until we could not ignore it. We had to take some action. Which, I think rather reluctantly, we did.

Or, rather, Jaworski did. We were empowered to act, but we were never going to. We wouldn't have except that Jaworski got the matter into court, so that we had the United States of America versus Richard Nixon the President of the United States. And then we had the tapes. When the Court ordered the revelation of the tapes, when it told the President that he could no longer keep those sequestered, that made the impeachment of Richard Nixon possible. Without the tapes we would have just been spinning our wheels. Without Jaworski, we would never have got to the matter, not even to the beginnings of impeachment.

Rodino called the Judiciary Committee together and said: "We are going to go into the matter of the impeachment of Richard Nixon."

The first order of business then was to hire competent counsel, which took awhile. The Democrats hired John Doar; the Republicans hired a lawyer from Chicago, Albert Jenner. And Doar and Jenner and the staff hired by them engaged in a lengthy in-depth investigation about what had been said and what had been done in terms of specific acts and whether they constituted a violation of the law. They compiled all of this into big black notebooks of reading material for us. And I gave credit for most of that to John Doar, who was an organizational genius.

So for weeks we met behind closed doors, going through these black notebooks. And the closed doors were legitimate, as the rules of the House said you did not have to have a public session if someone's character was to be discussed.

The big, major issue the committee had to deal with was how to define the charge. The Constitution said that the President shall be removed from office on impeachment for treason, bribery, or other high crimes and misdemeanors. So our job was to define "high crimes and misdemeanors," as that was the only reason that this President could be impeached. Meanwhile, I was studying all that, and also reading everything I could find, from any source, which had ever been written, said, or uttered about impeachment.

It was a funny time. Every day when we would leave those closed-door sessions the media people would chase us down the hall asking: "Have you found the smoking gun?"

After we finished going through all of the black note-books in the closed sessions, we went public with our information. We opened the doors and let the sunshine in. We invited the press. Rodino said: "This will be the format. Before we go into anything chargewise, offensewise, each person on the committee will have fifteen minutes to make an opening statement on television."

Now, there were thirty-five of us. And I recall that when Rodino said that, I thought: I don't think that's necessary. I said: "Lets deal with the issue and make a decision on the basis of the facts we have accumulated to this point. We don't need speechmaking." But I did not have much support for that position. The reaction from the other committee members was: "You must be out of your head." It seemed they all wanted that fifteen minutes on television.

The day we went public there were members who had been working on their opening statements for weeks, and I didn't have a word. I was still just reading my sources and trying to be sure that I understood the charge and the offenses. I was not going to vote to impeach Richard Nixon because I didn't like him. The knee-jerk thing. Because I figured that the easiest thing in the world would be for me to do just that, to say: "Yes, you ought to get out." So I was being extremely careful to review it all.

We arrived at the day for statements to begin, and the other people had prepared theirs, but I didn't have mine. I didn't intend to have an opening statement because I still didn't think that it was a good idea. All that speechmaking was a waste of the country's time, and the committee's time, and my time, was the way I felt about it then.

But of course it went right along as planned, with the committee members speaking all day and all night. It became apparent at some point that by the next evening they would get around to me, as we were proceeding by seniority. I was going to have to make a statement. Colleagues had come up to me all day to tell me: "I just can't wait to hear your opening statement. I want to hear what you have to say. I know you're going to let Nixon have it." I got this anticipation all day. One woman called up to say: "I have everything figured out. You're going to be on at nine o'clock and I'm having half a dozen people come over to my house so we can sit there and listen to you . . ."

So it was about five-thirty in the evening, and the Judiciary Committee was to reconvene at about eight-thirty. I went to my office and said to my assistant, Bud: "Would you believe the people who have come up to me today about my statement?" I was saying it in puzzlement; I knew there was nothing Bud could do about it. He asked; "Well, what are you going to say?" Now, Bud wanted to be perfectly clear that I really was coming out for impeachment. I told him: "Yes, I'm going to come out for impeachment. I have decided I am going to do that, and I am going to say why."

Then I told Marian Ricks, my secretary, "I know that you get off in fifteen minutes, but you're going to have to stay. I've got to write a statement, it seems." So while she was out there at her typewriter, I sat down at the desk in my office. It was now about six o'clock. I had all kinds of little disjointed notes that I'd written from all of my reading on impeachment. But I didn't have a statement. I had listened to statements for two days from other members. One thing that had struck me was how they had all started out by quoting the Preamble to the Constitution. Intoning about "We the People of the United States."

It occurred to me that not one of them had mentioned that back then the Preamble was not talking about *all* the people. So I said: "Well, I'll just start with that." I jotted down from this note and from that note and from this other note, and sent each page out to Marian when it was finished. I had already had my legislative assistant Bob Alcock parallel statements on impeachment—historical documents, Constitutions of the Confederacy, whenever impeachment had been talked about—against some of the offenses by Richard Nixon that we had talked about. So I also had that chart, that comparison about what had been said and what it was that Richard Nixon had done.

When I got in there, the Judiciary Committee was all seated and the camera was right there on us. We said what we had to say within our time span, and then we were through. The security was tight and no one applauded after you made a speech, so you didn't know how you had done.

On July 25, 1974, Barbara Jordan came before the television camera to present her position on the impeachment of the President of the United States. Solemn, tired, she hunched over four annotated amended pages of her own notes and four pages of historical impeachment criteria set against Nixon's actions.

Her black-rimmed glasses reflected the glare of the lights as she studied her notes. Then, improvising, she spoke to the unseen and unknown audience in living rooms across the country:

" 'We the people'—it is a very eloquent beginning. But when the Constitution of the United States was completed on the seventeenth of September in 1787, I was not included in that 'We the people.' I felt for many years that somehow George Washington and Alexander Hamilton just left me out by mistake. But through the process of amendment, interpretation, and court decision, I have finally been included in 'We the people.'

"Today I am an inquisitor. I believe hyperbole would not be fictional and would not overstate the solemnness that I feel right now. My faith in the Constitution is whole. It is complete. It is total. I am not going to sit here and be an idle spectator to the diminution, the subversion, the destruction of the Constitution.

" 'Who can so properly be the inquisitors for the nation as the representatives of the nation themselves?' (*The Federalist Papers*, No. 65). 'The subject of its jurisdiction are those offenses which proceed from the misconduct of public men.' In other words, the jurisdiction comes from the abuse or violation of some public trust.

"It is wrong, I suggest, it is a misreading of the Constitution for any member here to assert that for a member to vote for an Article of Impeachment means that the member must be convinced that the President should be removed from office. The Constitution doesn't say that. The powers relating to impeachment are an essential check in the hands of this body, the legislature, against and upon the encroachment of the Executive. In establishing the division between the two branches of the legislature, the House and the Senate, assigning to one the right to accuse and the other the right to judge, the framers of this Constitution were very astute. They did not make the accusers and the judges the same persons.

"We know the nature of impeachment. We have been talking about it for a while now. 'It is chiefly designed for the President and his high ministers' to somehow be called into account. It is designed to 'bridle' the Executive if he engages in excesses. It is designed as a method of national 'inquest into the conduct of public men' (*Federalist*, No. 65). The framers confined in the Congress the power, if need be, to remove the President in order to strike a delicate balance between a President swollen with power and grown tyrannical, and preservation of the independence of the Executive. The nature of impeachment is a narrowly channeled exception to the separation of powers maxim; the Federal Convention of 1787 said that. It limited impeachment to 'high crimes and misdemeanors' and discounted and opposed the term 'maladministration.' It is to be used only for great misdemeanors, so it was said in the North Carolina ratification convention. And in the Virginia ratification convention: 'We do not trust liberty to a particular branch. We need one branch to check the others.'

" 'No one need be afraid' it was said in the North Carolina ratification convention; 'No one need be afraid that officers who commit oppression will pass with immunity.'

" 'Prosecutions of impeachments will seldom fail to agitate the passions of the whole community,' said Hamilton in the *Federalist Papers*, No. 65, 'and to divide it into parties more or less friendly or inimical to the accused.' I do not mean political parties in that sense.

"The drawing of political lines goes to the motivation behind impeachment; but impeachment must proceed within the confines of the constitutional term 'high crimes and misdemeanors.'

"Of the impeachment process, it was Woodrow Wilson who said that 'nothing short of the grossest offenses against the plain law of the land will suffice to give them speed and effectiveness. Indignation so great as to overgrow party interest may secure a conviction; nothing else can.'

"Common sense would be revolted if we engaged upon this process for petty reasons. Congress has a lot to do: appropriations, tax reform, health insurance, campaign finance reform, housing, environmental protection, energy sufficiency, mass transportation. Pettiness cannot be allowed to stand in the face of such overwhelming problems. So today we are not being petty. We are trying to be big because the talk we have before us is a big one.

"This morning, in a discussion of the evidence, we are told that the evidence which purports to support the allegations of misuse of the CIA by the President is thin. We are told that the evidence is insufficient. What that recital of the evidence this morning did not include is what the President did know on June 23, 1972. The President did know that it was Republican money, that it was money from the Committee for the Re-election of the President, which was found in the possession of one of the burglars arrested on June 17.

"What the President did know on the twenty-third of June was the prior activities of E. Howard Hunt, which included his participation in the break-in of Daniel Ellsberg's psychiatrist, which included Howard Hunt's participation in the Dita Beard ITT affair, which included Howard Hunt's fabrication of cables, designed to discredit the Kennedy administration.

"We were further cautioned today that perhaps these proceedings ought to be delayed because certainly there would be new evidence forthcoming from the President of the United States. There has not even been an obfuscated indication that this committee would receive any additional materials from the President. The committee subpoena is outstanding, and if the President wants to supply that material, the committee sits here.

"The fact is that yesterday, the American people waited with great anxiety for eight hours, not knowing whether their President would obey an order of the Supreme Court of the United States.

"At this point I would like to juxtapose a few of the impeachment criteria with some of the President's actions:

"James Madison said in the Virginia Ratification Convention: 'If the President be connected in any suspicious manner with any person and there be grounds to believe that he will shelter him, he may be impeached.'

"We have heard time and time again that the evidence reflects payment to the defendants of money. The President has knowledge that these funds were being paid and that these were funds collected for the 1972 presidential campaign.

"We know that the President met with [Assistant Attorney General] Henry Petersen twenty-seven times to discuss matters related to Watergate, and immediately thereafter met with the very persons who were implicated in the information Mr. Petersen was receiving and transmitting to the President. Madison's words again: 'If the President be connected in any suspicious manner with any person and there be grounds to believe that he will shelter that person, he may be impeached.'

"Justice Story: 'Impeachment is intended for occasional and extraordinary cases where a superior power acting for the whole people is put into operation to protect their rights and rescue their liberties from violation.'

"We know about the break-in at the psychiatrist's office.

We know that there was absolute complete direction in August, 1971, when the President instructed Ehrlichman to 'do whatever is necessary.' This instruction led to a surreptitious entry into Dr. Fielding's office . . .

"The South Carolina Ratification Convention impeachment criteria: Those are impeachable 'who behave amiss or betray their public trust.'

"Beginning shortly after the Watergate break-in and continuing to the present time, the President has engaged in a series of public statements and actions designed to thwart the lawful investigation by government prosecutors. Moreover, the President has made public announcements and assertions bearing on the Watergate case which the evidence will show he knew to be false . . .

"James Madison said, again at the Constitutional Convention: 'A President is impeachable if he attempts to subvert the Constitution.'

"The Constitution charges that President with the task of taking care that the laws be faithfully executed, and yet the President has counseled his aides to commit perjury, willfully disregarded the secrecy of grand jury proceedings, concealed surreptitious entry, attempted to compromise a federal judge while publicly displaying his cooperation with the processes of criminal justice . . .

"If the impeachment provision in the Constitution of the United States will not reach the offenses charged here, then perhaps that eighteenth-century Constitution should be abandoned to a twentieth-century paper shredder. Has the President committed offenses and planned and directed and acquiesced in a course of conduct which the Constitution will not tolerate? That is the question. We know that. We know the question. We should now forthwith proceed to answer the question. It is reason and not passion which must guide our deliberations, guide our debate, and guide our decision."

Her audience sat stunned. It was the first time she had reached them with no one in between. The first time they had seen and heard her with their own eyes and ears. The first time she was a primary source to them.

Before that, she had long since been stereotyped by a press used to summing up secondary sources. Typical was a feature in the liberal Austin newspaper the *Texas Observer* (November 1972):

"The Fifth Ward is . . . your just average crummy Southern ghetto . . . She accepted 98 per cent of what her father taught her . . . She went on to Boston University Law School, the only woman in a class of 128 . . . She decided to become a lawyer when she was in the tenth grade and a woman named Edith Sampson came to address Phyllis Wheatley High School Career Day Assembly. Sampson was a lawyer . . . Where did the voice come from? Like everything else about Jordan, it was always there . . . Aside from the vicarious kick a white lib can get from watching Jordan speak to a new audience—they tend to snigger and assume that anyone who looks that much like a mammy is going to be pretty funny to hear—she's not much use as a token . . . Even the people who have broken through her fierce sense of privacy are not sure of the friendship."

The night of the impeachment hearings, Barbara broke through her interpreters. Thereafter, to her audience, she would be a myth of their own creating, an institution, a legend accountable to their prejudgment. Thereafter she would be public property, would be a folk-hero. But on that single evening she reached America one to one.

In an outpouring of letters her listeners opened up to her their feelings, adoring and despising, and their words, eloquent and awkward.

A man in Houston the next day went out and put up twenty-five billboards that said: THANK YOU, BARBARA JORDAN, FOR EXPLAINING THE CONSTITUTION TO US.

"You know why you are such a forceful speaker, because you are honest. I have wished I was colored so I could be honest. Sometimes I feel I may have been a person in another time who belonged to the oppressed . . ."

"Your remarks on President Nixon were much too amusing to take seriously. You should beg God to forgive you for your part in attempting to destroy a great man. As for the truth of what you say, your arrogance is exceeded only by your ignorance . . ."

"I am nine years old. I am all for impeachment. I think President Nixon will be impeached. I think you should run for President."

"The stationery may not be very good, but the sentiment we feel for you is.

"We are an average American middle-class family who have been on top, and plunged to the bottom, and made a remarkable comeback. White, Lutheran, middle class, and we must say we have been very moved, very impressed, and so happy we saw and learned to know you on the Watergate hearings on television . . ."

"I wish to thank you for your support of the impeachment of President Nixon. Your fifteen-minute statement to the committee was a literary masterpiece in my estimation. Granted that past administrations may have been corrupt also, Nixon's venality must be terminated here and now if my thirteen-year-old son is to inherit any semblance of decent government. As a naturalized citizen I have tasted but a small portion of the discrimination your people suffered. Change is never easy. There is always a price tag on it. Again I thank you for the price you had to pay. Good luck to you."

"All of us who love all of the Mosaic of this precious land that is our own bless you for your Forceful, Scholarly, Eloquent and Epic statement of the case. Now you belong to the ages. 'Free at last.'"

"I am not from Texas, nor am I black. Probably I am best described as a cynical and disillusioned observer of the American political process.

"For the first time in quite a while, I am encouraged. My optimism, though guarded, is engendered as a consequence of your opening statement of 25 July, during the House Judiciary Committee impeachment debate.

"Eloquence, forthrightness, incisive rationality, and dignity are rare qualities. Yet you, as a black woman from the South, vividly displayed these qualities. That a black woman from the South should have these qualities is no surprise; that the American political process should have

progressed far enough to allow you to display these qualities to the entire country is a surprise . . ."

"In order to work with the male colleagues in our Capitol
it isn't necessary to use the attitude you did—a cocky
know-it-all one; you are very intelligent, so you don't have
to resort to an obnoxious projection."

"Madam, after Listen to you in Impeachment Committee which you speak so eloquence made me Happy. Because I was Born in Texas in 1874, 9 of June. I know you
had some Bad Days to make it where you are to Day. Since
we are so far apart I am asking you to send me one of your
poto that I mite keep it the Rest of My Life."

"I think your a nice person plus a wonderful attorney. I
would like to see Tricky Dick brought to trial. I think
theirs more to be told."

"Have heard many speeches from politicians and listened to them reprove many things but never has anyone
run down the Founding Fathers as you did. They may not
have had you in mind when they set up the original structure of our country but you look as if you have fared extremely well in our system, so why don't you just shut up
and quit crying in your beer and eliminate this self-
pity? . . ."

"I am 48 years old, black, female, I was born in a mining
town in rural Alabama. This should give you an idea of
some of the circumstances of my early years as well as my
growing-up process. Nevertheless, I have earned a doctor-

ate degree and have held respectable administrative positions during my professional career. I have known many
outstanding people—Mrs. Mary McLeod Bethune, Dr.
Martin Luther King, Jr., Whitney M. Young, Jr., Roy
Wilkins—all, in my estimation, the epitomes of the dedicated, concerned, active black. Last night, I met you . . ."

"I followed the televised Judiciary Committee hearings
very closely and was most impressed with your cogency,
articulation, and probity. You simply made me proud to be
an American . . . I was very moved by your opening
remarks . . . quite to tears. Run for President someday and
I shall be there with you! . . ."

"Wish I was in your district. My representative he don't
do nothing. Double negative and I don't care."

"I sincerely hope when many of you politicians in
Washington, D.C., finish that we will still have something
left of our government; the Communists must laugh with
joy at what is taking place, and the American taxpayers are
picking up the tab."

"What a pleasure and privilege to listen to you. Your
eloquence, your brilliant mind, and above all your
magnificent voice—what a voice—to me your voice is like
listening to the most brilliant symphony. Everyone should
have the opportunity to hear your voice—"

"I loved to here you speak. You are a Beautiful Woman,
we watch on TV. We only hope we get someone in the

White House that is a Democratic, and I work in our neighborhood. I am 74 years old and my husband is 83 and I work every day. But we want to thank all of you good people for our good USA. I am a white lady that love you all."

"This white, Yankee Republican would be honored at some future date to campaign for our 1st black, 1st woman President. If you were the candidate.

"My Republican President has let me down plus most of my Republican Congressmen.

"Do not weary of your task. We need your honest, forceful voice."

"My wife and I were both extremely proud of our Texas Congresswoman when we listened to your presentation last night. We don't know what the final end to this problem is yet, but I'll bet one thing: it'll scare the hell out of anyone in the White House in the future when such monkey business is mentioned."

"I have a picture of you and was wondering if you could sign it. Also, if you are running for re-election, could you send me a few different kinds of buttons?"

"I guess you will be surprised at hearing from a person not all prominent, just a lady who heard your address on the T.V. Never at a loss for words, you showed everyone up on the committee.

"I worked for President Johnson in '65. On my day away from work I rang doorbells and passed out his cards. I have always been interested in my country. Just stay in there, you are on the right side. I have talked to so many people and you were warmly and greatly admired."

"My maiden name was Jordan. My father's family trace ancestry to Thomas Jordan of England who came to Virginia about 1700. The name of Samuel Jordan is a monument at Jamestown . . . Naturally I am interested to know how far back you trace your ancestry."

"God Bless you Honey! You were wonderful! I never was more proud of womanhood than in her shining hour, fighting for the rights, privileges, and principles all of us Americans should have a right to . . . As the mother of six children on an inadequate salary facing the devastating escalation of goods, living costs, I look to my President for an example and see nothing! Impounding of economic aid, unemployment rampant, big business corporations profiteering at our expense. Dear God, if we care about our country and its future this gross abuse must stop!"

"When you speak of that great Document the 'Constitution of our beloved United States' it brings tears to my eyes. You see I am European born and a citizen by 'choice.' I pledged to protect and allegiance to it, not to the President, whoever he may be. Your vote is not against a President but Richard M Nixon who consorts with the enemy of the Constitution, which spells Treason in any language."

"You have changed the minds of myself, my wife, our relatives, and all our friends, for the good of our country, as before we watched you on T.V. we thought only a man should be the President but all of us will vote for you or any black man or lady."

"Your scholarship was breathtaking tonight; your logic convincing; your sincerity unimpeachable; your power and beauty and dignity overwhelming. When you run for President, you can count on my vote."

"I am so proud to be your friend. When your time came, you were ready."

When the Judiciary Committee adjourned that night, and we had all made our speeches, Bud came and said: "Come on, your car's outside." And just as we approached the front door of the Rayburn Building, there was this big crowd of people standing over there and it looked like they were just all around my car. And I said: "Uh-oh, what is that?" I said to Bud: "The only thing we can do is walk over to my car, get in, and drive away, and not say anything to anybody and not look right and not look left." Well, when I walked out the front door, they broke into this big cheer—screaming, "Right on!" and waving fists in the air. And someone said: "I knew that when you talked you were going to base whatever you were going to say on the law, if you had to go back to Moses." And that was the first reaction I had to my speech.

I think they liked it that I didn't present a harangue, but that I was very serious about what I was doing. I felt that was what I was communicating. That here was a person who had really thought this through and had reached a decision, a considered, sincere, and sensible decision.

But I didn't like the idea of working to impeach a President. I didn't like doing that; I wished that it had not been necessary to do that. I really did. We had great difficulty trying to frame articles of impeachment, and the first vote on the first article of impeachment in committee was very painful for me. When the roll was called and I was asked, "How do you vote?" I could barely get my "yes" out. And after that vote, about three or four of us on the committee went back into one of the council rooms and there were tears. We had to let out our feelings.

But when our articles of impeachment were voted ultimately by the Judiciary Committee and we were to present this indictment to the Senate, I wanted to be one of the managers on the part of the House who did that.

But of course I never got a chance. Nobody did. Because Nixon resigned. Which was a mixture of relief that we didn't have to go forward with it, and disappointment because due process did not take place. And it should have.

Mostly I felt it unfair that Mr. Nixon and his counsel had lied to the Judiciary Committee for so long. Nixon's counsel had been there for rebuttal after we completed our deliberations, and we kept asking about various things and they denied them. Then, after Nixon resigned and everything caved in, he admitted to them. The members of the Judiciary Committee who had been supportive of him all went on television and said they were sorry that they had made a mistake. So he had lied to us; and I regretted that.

Before this, Agnew had resigned, and we had gone through the confirmation of Gerald Ford for Vice President. During the time Ford was questioned for his confirmation I had decided that I could not vote for him because I did not feel he had the capacity to become the President.

After Nixon had resigned and Ford had become President, I got this call from someone saying that the President would like for me to go to China with a group. I said: "To China?" He said: "Peking, the People's Republic of China. You know Nixon made the approach," he said. "He went to Peking, and the Shanghai Communiqué was signed at that point, and now Nixon is out and we are trying to show continuity of policy by showing that, even though we have put Richard Nixon out of office, that does not change anything about what was developed as policy toward the People's Republic."

I asked him: "Who else is going?" He said: "Well, Senator Fulbright, Senator Humphrey." He named the whole crew. So I said: "Let me think about this. That's quite a distance to travel. I will have to think about it. But it's a good crowd to be traveling with." And I thought about it for a couple of days, and I said: "Yes."

So I went. And then there we were in China in some little province just at the foot of a mountain and sleeping on these slatted cots with straw mats, when I got a knock at my door and they said: "We have a telephone call for you." I said: "Well, one moment." And I put on a robe and some slippers and went down to this little funny-looking telephone and said into it: "Hello." Then there was this voice from Channel Thirteen in Houston wanting to know: "What do you think about Ford's pardon of Richard Nixon?"

I said: "What the hell are you talking about? What?" I said: "Now wait a minute, just repeat what you have said. Slowly." And he repeated it to me, and I said: "Well, did

Nixon plead guilty or something?" I couldn't get it all together. Couldn't understand that the President had sent all of us as far out of the country as possible to this little province so this could happen. And that's where I heard about it for the first time.

Well, when we got back to the States, of course, that was all that was in the news, and although it was obvious that Ford could do that—there was no constitutional prohibition—well, I felt cheated. I said: "Something at least could have been resolved with the finality of a court decision, but now everything is wiped out."

The country definitely got short-changed. I don't know whether it would have been the long, agonizing nightmare which Gerald Ford said it would be for the country if we had gone through the trial. But I do know that it would have been done with finality.

So that was the end of impeachment.

8. ENTRENCHMENT

Operating always in the present moment, Barbara in Congress was wholly in Congress.

Which meant that all her time not spent on the floor under the etched eagle, surrounded by the blue damask walls, shepherding her legislation and reacting to that of others, was spent reading reams of related material, in order to gain the perspective she felt others must somehow have. She retained the feeling she had had at Boston University that she must work harder than the rest to make up for what she did not know. "If there is an issue on the floor of the Congress, a big one, then I am interested in the historical background of that issue because that helps me to understand where we are now. I send over to the Library of Congress to get the simplest things. I want to be steeped in what we are discussing. I think that there are people who already know that information, but I don't. So I'm doing background for legislation all the time."

Her office staff operated chiefly to locate and provide her constant demand for research materials—and to keep the public at bay. Barbara's salary, over ten times what it had been in the Texas Legislature, could be supplemented by honorariums only up to $25,000 a year, and, as her maximum fee was $2,000 a speech, this served to help her cull from thousands of requests only those public appearances that dealt with matters currently of interest to her.

Old friends, assuming a continuity of past she did not share, found it difficult to comprehend being placed in the same category with the general seeker after her presence. Charles White, her companion from afternoons after school spent walking down the Lyons Avenue of their common youth, called from a radio station in Ohio to ask her to speak to a Planned Parenthood group; Issie Shelton, co-survivor of Boston University Law School, now counsel for the Equal Employment Opportunities Commission, wanted her to come have dinner with a collection of prominent Washington blacks; Louise Bailey, seeking to be remembered as the first white friend, asked her to speak to a community-wide meeting in Hartford and added the promise of a private plane to get Barbara to her next appointment. All of these reached out to her from yesterday to find themselves, whether their requests were accepted or rejected, not a part of her world today.

Those in the present, on the other hand, had free access to her time. When Congressman Mahon, Chairman of the Appropriations Committee, interrupted her on another phone call to ask if she would sing with him at the West Texas Chamber of Commerce meeting, she was jocular and glad to oblige. Doing favors was part and parcel of the ongoing business of doing business in the Congress of the United States.

Inevitably, her primary concern—minority legislation—reflected her present conviction that where she was she owed to the law; that no amount of confidence and determination could win elections without redistricting and reapportionment; that discriminatory voting practices and segregated public accommodations could close doors that only the law could open.

In 1973, the first session of her first term, the Omnibus Crime Control and Safe Streets Act came up for renewal. Barbara decided that this act, as it came through the Judiciary Committee for review, would be a good vehicle for her first legislation.

Passed in 1968, this act had created the Law Enforcement Assistance Administration (LEAA) for the purpose of assisting state and local governments in their law-enforcement activities to reduce crime. It set out to develop initiatives for citizens to participate in fighting crime; to use its discretionary funds to attack criminal-case backlog and delay; to develop standards and criteria for programs to improve state and local correctional facilities; and to focus attention on funding programs to reduce crime against the elderly.

As originally passed, it had no civil rights provisions, and that was the discrepancy Barbara decided to attack. Working out what became known as the Jordan Amendment, Barbara proposed to mandate the use of federal funds in a nondiscriminatory fashion.

Having taken the amendment through the subcommittee and the whole committee, she retained it on the floor of the House, where it passed. After it came out of the Senate in substantially different form and was sent to conference committee, Barbara was appointed a conferee—unusual for a freshman member—as she had proposed the original wording.

Rodino, Chairman of the Judiciary Committee, had suggested to her that she might have trouble getting her version by Senator McClellan (D., Ark.), who headed the conference committee. "Place me right beside him," she requested, "so he will have to deal with me directly."

In committee session, McClellan, the chairman, kept passing over her amendment, saying that they would get back to it later. Finally, when he was worn down, Barbara got to speak to it, explaining that everybody there knew that federal money was not spent equally and that everybody there knew that it should be. McClellan asked: "But isn't this already the law?" To which she replied: "Well, certainly, Senator, it's already the law. But there are some of these jurisdictions behaving as if they don't know it's the law. So why don't we just spell it out here for them?"

"Now, we're not going in there and just cut off money for a lot of people, are we?" McClellan asked.

"The way they avoid getting any money cut off is just to obey the law, Senator . . ."

So the Jordan Amendment was passed, and inserted into the extended LEAA bill, reading:

"(c) (1) No person in any State shall on the ground of race, color, national origin, or sex be excluded from participation in, be denied the benefits of, or be subjected to discrimination under any program or activity funded in whole or in part with funds made available under this title."

Insuring that it had a certain method of enforcement, it continued:

"(c) (2) Whenever the Adminstration determines that a State government or any unit of general local government has failed to comply with subsection (c) (1) or an applicable regulation, it shall notify the chief executive of the State of the noncompliance and shall request the chief executive to secure compliance. If, within a reasonable time after such notification, the chief executive fails or refuses to secure compliance, the Administration shall exercise the powers and functions provided in section 509 of this title and is authorized concurrently with such exercises—

"(A) to institute an appropriate civil action

"(B) to exercise the powers and functions pursuant to Title VI of the Civil Rights Act of 1964 (42 U.S. 2000d); or

"(C) take such other action as may be provided by law.

"(3) Whenever the Attorney General has reason to believe that a State government or unit of local government is engaged in a pattern or practice in violation of the provisions of this section the Attorney General may bring a civil action in any appropriate United States district court for such relief as may be appropriate, including injunctive relief."

In her second term, learning that the LEAA was not working as she had intended, she built in an enforcement process for notification of denying jurisdictions funds if discrimination were proved. She also, on the Government Operations Committee, extended similar civil rights provisions to a revenue-sharing bill.

In addition, under the Monopolies and Commercial Law Subcommittee of the Judiciary Committee, she introduced a bill proposing the repeal of the Fair Trade laws, which allowed manufacturers to establish a price for a product and enforce that price in retail sales. In her mind, this was a price-fixing mechanism which prevented free competition, and therefore hurt minority-run businesses. Originally it had been seen as a device to help the small, independent owner, the "Mom and Pop" stores. "I don't know whether Mom and Pop ever heard of the bill, but at least they didn't show up to testify. Only the big manufacturer came to protest my bill."

Rodino let her manage this bill on the floor of the House, and, after it passed both houses overwhelmingly in the same language, she got to keep the pen with which President Ford signed the bill. "That's what you do up here—you collect pens."

Most important of her civil rights work was her extension of the Voting Rights Act. She considered that the right to vote, that basic right of citizenship, had been effectively prohibited blacks in various covert, convoluted ways since they were given it in the Fifteenth Amendment.

As Burke Marshall, Assistant Attorney General for Civil Rights under Kennedy, had expressed it (*Federalism and Civil Rights*): "Only political power—not court orders or other federal law—will insure the election of fair men as sheriffs, school board members, police chiefs, mayors, county commissioners, and state officials. It is they who control the institutions which grant or deny federally guaranteed rights . . . Any elected official represents not the people in his district, but the people in his district who vote."

Barbara remembered that Johnson, when he was President, had said that even more than we have to ensure that everybody can go to the bathroom and eat without harassment we must determine that all people have equal franchisement.

Under him, after the civil rights marches in Selma and

Montgomery, the original Voting Rights Act of 1965 was passed, stating:

"No voting qualification or prerequisite to voting, or standard, practice, or procedure shall be imposed or applied by any State or political subdivision to deny or abridge the right of any citizen of the United States to vote on account of race or color."

Additionally, the act stated that:

"[N]o citizen shall be denied the right to vote in any Federal, State, or local election because of his failure to comply with any test or device . . ."

This had put an end to such subterfuges as formidable application-to-vote forms required only of blacks, or difficult literacy tests requiring only blacks to define such terms as *ex post facto* and *habeas corpus*, or the financially discriminating poll tax, which Texas had used.

This original bill had been targeted only at the Deep South states, and therefore Texas had been excluded. But Barbara had begun to receive a continual flood of complaints concerning voting obstructions and intimidation in heavily black East Texas, and from Mexican Americans who had difficulty reading the English-printed ballots. She decided, when the Voting Rights Act came up for review, that Texas should be brought under its coverage.

In 1975, she introduced an amendment to the bill's renewal—that Texas be placed under its jurisdiction. She claimed that if a given percentage of the population had a language other than English, that ballots only in English would constitute a test or device, and therefore be a violation of the Voting Rights Act.

Every elected official in the state opposed the idea of including Texas. Because under the Act if you made any change in election requirements or procedures, that change would have to be approved by the Attorney General of the United States before it could go into effect, and if complaints were made of discrimination in voting procedures, the Justice Department could send federal registrars into an area with jurisdiction to handle the election. State officials were aghast. *Federales* would be intruding into local elections.

The legislature hastily voted compulsory bilingual ballots, in an effort to block Texas' inclusion under the act.

Meanwhile, following Barbara's plan, the 1975 Congress expanded its definition of "test or device" to include:

"Any practice or requirement by which any State or political subdivision provided any registration or voting notices, forms, instructions, assistance, or other materials or information relating to the electoral process, including ballots, only in the English language, where the Director of the Census determines that more than five per centum of the citizens of voting age residing in such State or political subdivision are members of a single language minority."

Under this new language-minority provision, in order to permit enforcement, the Director of the Census had to prove that more than 5 per cent of the voting-age citizens of the state belonged to a single-language minority (American Indian, Asian American, Alaskan native, persons of "Spanish heritage"). The Director was to determine that on November 1, 1972, in the last presidential election, less than 50 per cent of the voting-age citizens were registered to vote, or less than 50 per cent of the voting-age citizens actually voted. And the Attorney General was to make a separate determination as to whether the state had maintained a "test or device" as of November 1972.

Texas, fighting this all the way, took the case to court in

1976. Secretary of State Mark White challenged the state's inclusion, claiming error on all three determinations. He claimed that the fact that 5 per cent of the voting-age population was of Spanish heritage was unrealistic because of the large number of illegal aliens; that the fact that 50 per cent of the voters did not vote did not prove it was Mexican Americans who had not voted; and that the all-English election of November 1972 should not be considered a test, as the state legislature had now made all-English elections illegal.

But the Supreme Court held unanimously that Texas was subject to the Voting Rights Act; and, to make matters worse in the eyes of Texans, through a fluke the newly included states were to be covered for longer than those states whose eligibility had been renewed from the old act of 1965.

When Barbara's bill passed the House, it had been privately agreed by the Senate leadership that when the physical bill itself got to the Senate, it would be held at the desk for the members to consider directly without sending it to committee, as they feared Senator Eastland, conservative Mississippi head of the Senate Judiciary Committee, would block it.

So, when the Senate was debating it on the floor, what they were actually debating was a piece of paper which said the Senate agrees to the House bill. After several weeks of filibustering, Senator Robert Byrd (D., W.Va.) put together a compromise to end discussion. His suggestion was for an extension for seven years instead of ten. However, when passed, due to the way the insertions were made in the House bill, the existing Deep South states were only covered for another seven years, while the new states (including the Spanish-speaking counties in Texas, Florida, California, New Mexico, and Arizona) were covered for a full ten, until August 1985.

Unlike the original Civil Rights Act of 1965, in which the individual had to file a suit to get relief from discrimination, the new Voting Rights Act, due in part to Barbara's efforts, provided for suits brought by the U. S. Attorney General as well. This was because, although the right to vote had existed for blacks since 1869, virtually no individual suits had been brought. Which, in the absence of federal monitoring, had made it difficult to control incidents attempting to bar blacks from polling places, or economic retaliation against blacks who did attempt to vote.

Barbara enjoyed bucking the whole state of Texas on this matter. "I was hanging in there. And I wouldn't kneel."

She also enjoyed the flourishing of another presidential pen, this time on a bill Ford had been most reluctant to sign, a bill that, against his will, had become an accomplished fact.

Doggedly reading from typed cards, in the rose garden of the White House, the President gave his belated endorsement to the new Voting Rights Act:

— I am pleased today to sign HR 6219, which extends and broadens the provisions of the Voting Rights Act of 1965. The right to vote is at the very foundation of our American system of government—and nothing must interfere with this precious right.
— Today is the tenth anniversary of the signing by President Johnson of the Voting Rights Act of 1965, which I supported. In the past decade the voting rights of millions of Americans have been protected and our system of government has been strengthened immeasurably.

— The bill I am signing today extends the temporary provisions of the act for seven more years and broadens these provisions to bar discrimination against Spanish-speaking Americans, American Indians, Alaskan natives, and Asian Americans.

— Further, this bill will permit private citizens as well as the Attorney General to initiate suits to protect voting rights of citizens in any state where discrimination occurs.

— There must be no question about the right of each eligible citizen to participate in our elective process. The extension of this act will help ensure that right.

Barbara recounted that moment. "I was in Texas and we were in a recess, but I thought it was worth flying back to Washington to make sure Gerald Ford got his name on that bill. Ford had fought it in the Senate, but he decided that the battle was lost. So he had a stack of three-by-five cards and he read about how he had worked for its successful passage, and I said: 'Your remarks are most interesting.' And he perked up and said: 'Would you like to have them?' And I said: 'Certainly, Mr. President.' So I fixed up a display of my get-together with Ford over those little cards."

If Barbara's work for civil rights came from the gut, from the conviction still present to her that only through legal changes could minorities gain equality, her reaction to women's rights was more ambiguous.

Not having been married, she had not dealt firsthand with such chattel-status matters as credit discrimination or loss of contractual autonomy. Reading the definition of slavery in the Civil Rights decision of 1883—"compulsory service of the slave for the benefit of the master, restraint of his movements except by the master's will, disability to hold property, to make contracts, to have a standing in court"—she was not reminded of the early lot of women. Not having borne infants, she did not interpolate how it might feel to have no control over whether or not your body reproduced.

She could, and did, intellectually endorse and vote for such advances as the Equal Rights Amendment and federal aid for abortion; but personally she felt that any female could, as she had, exercise without impediment those choices necessary for success. She assumed that any woman who made the same single-minded decision to give career first priority that she had, could excel. For this reason, women's progress seemed more a matter of attitude to her than a matter of law.

On the floor of the Congress, she did what needed to be done. In her third term, when the House was debating the Hyde Amendment to the HEW Labor Appropriations Bill, which said that the federal government may not use any of its moneys for abortions, she swung what votes she could. Going up to Jim Wright, the majority leader, just as he was about to vote "yes" for the House position, she intercepted him as he put his finger on the button. "Now, let's just think about the alternatives available here. The Senate position is that this is all right when the life of the mother is at stake. You know we're not going to have people who are not qualified to make a decision as to whether abortion is medically necessary. It would hurt me greatly if you can't see the wisdom of this." And Wright, stared down by her, changed his vote.

Arguing with her colleagues on the Judiciary Committee about the proposal to extend ratification of the Equal Rights Amendment for a second seven years, she defended it heatedly. "Mr. Chairman, this has not been an easy

morning for some of us. I regret that fourteen years is repugnant as a time frame for ratification for some members
of this committee. Fourteen years is not repugnant to me. A
generation is not repugnant to me. Who am I to say let's
short circuit the time during which I may seek to protect
and guarantee my personhood in the community of human-
kind. I can't restrict that and certainly no constitutional
scholar can restrict that."

But her internal reaction to such debates was not as
clear-cut. "I guess the most disastrous argument I've ever
heard on the floor of the House was that abortion debate.
It was awful the people who got up and sermonized. It was
a super mess. We, the sixteen women in the House, were
trying to orchestrate the whole thing. We had these
clowns on the floor talking, and one man looked like he
was pregnant, and he was ranting around. And I couldn't
take any more of it. I told one of my female colleagues:
'I'm going to the ladies' lounge and read a book, and if you
need me in this debate that's where I'll be.' And I just left."

During the International Women's Year, at a conference
at the LBJ School of Public Affairs in Austin, November
10, 1975, Barbara gave a speech that summarized her thinking on the injustices done women and on their own ability
to lift themselves by force of will to equality:

" . . . I'm delighted that I could come here to this conference which is dedicated to the liberation of men. If you
had to work in the environment of Washington, D.C., as
I do, and watch those men who are so imprisoned and so
confined by their eighteenth-century thought patterns,
you would know that if anybody is going to be liberated,
it's men who must be liberated in this country.

" . . . In 1975, International Women's Year, it is very

easy for all of us to be optimistic about the advances of women. We can talk about social advancement, educational advances, economic justice coming to women. But we know that the government of the United States of America remains so sharply focused on problems of inflation and recession and depression and unemployment that it is unlikely that issues related to women will receive any primacy of attention.

". . . In this country, we have climbed over some of the legal obstacles which affect women. We have gotten around some of those social and educational obstacles, barriers, and moved ahead to opportunity in those areas. But there can be no letup. There can be no slackening of effort, because we still must keep a momentum building, growing, sustained.

"The progress of the Equal Rights Amendment is good. But we are still four states short . . . The amendment is so simple, that in all of the negative rhetoric which you have heard about it, some of us who are for the amendment have had to go back and read it and see exactly what it is that it says. It's very simple: 'Equality of rights under the law shall not be denied or abridged by the United States or by any other state on account of sex.'

"Now, to me, that is stated in plain, simple, ordinary English. Yet there are those who have great difficulty understanding what those words mean . . . Now, when the amendment was first approved by the Congress, it appeared that within at least a year the necessary ratification would have occurred. At that time of the approval by the Congress, I was a member of the Senate of this state. We had as our lieutenant governor, Ben Barnes.

"You remember Ben Barnes? You see, it was at that time that Ben thought he was on his way to the White House.

Something happened on the way. But suffice it to say, when Congress approved that amendment, Ben was in a great hurry, a grand rush, for the State of Texas to be the first state in the Union to grant its approval.

"And, as a member of the Senate over which he presided, I was given the task of pushing that amendment through. He said: 'Let's hurry up. We need to be No. 1.' Well, we hurried up but we were not number one.

"Now if you were to try to get that amendment ratified and approved by the legislature of this state today can't you see the difficult task we'd have? In the first place, we'd have to call in a Constitutional expert to explain it to the governor. Now, that was unfair of me to say that. Because I've heard that the governor knows how to read—

" . . . But, think about some of the things which have been said about that amendment by in-state legislative bodies where the amendment is not yet approved. Now, just listen to this. I think the language is classic:

"In Maryland, for example, there was a minister testifying against the amendment and he said that the 'supporters of the amendment are products of unhappy homes, unhappy marriages, unhappy parents, and they are to be pitied.' That was what he said.

"And in Virginia a woman told the legislature, listen to this, a *woman:* 'Please don't make us stoop to equality; we love being treated with superiority.'

"In Georgia, a state representative called the amendment 'so stinking of Communism, it's just pitiful to think of doing something like that to America.' He said, and this is the same enlightened gentleman, speaking before the legislature of the State of Georgia, 'That amendment would lower our ladies to the level of men.'

"Now, I don't know how those words of the proposed

amendment can be so misconstrued, but they can be. The problem remains, my friends who are assembled here, the problem remains that we have difficulty defining ourselves. The problem remains that we fail to define ourselves in terms of whole human beings, full human beings. We reduce the definition of our lives just a little bit because somewhere in the back of our minds is the thought that we really are not quite equal. In spite of what we say, there is, at some level, in most of us, the thought that we are not yet quite equal. That's nobody's fault but ours, because, even though we talk a good game, we don't really act out the equality we say we feel.

"Several years ago, Secretary General U Thant of the United Nations issued a report. The title of the report is so long, I'll have to read it: 'Implementation of the Declaration on the Elimination of Discrimination Against Women.' A long title, but the findings are quite interesting.

"The report summarized the replies received from thirty-nine governments on national trends in regard to the rights of women, both in compliance with the law and compliance with the principles of this declaration.

"In this report, the Secretary General wrote these words: '. . . In light of the information received, it is clear that among the major stumbling blocks in the path to the full *de facto* realization of the rights of women, irrespective of the degree of national development, are the traditional concepts of the roles men and women must assume in the family, in the community, and in the society at large.'

"What the Secretary General was saying, in effect, is that it is that assumed traditional role which, more than anything else, has to do with impediments to the achievement of the rights of women.

"There is a study by a Cornell University economics professor, Marjorie Galenson. She demonstrates some of the faults of this traditional conceptualization of the roles of women by women. Professor Galenson demonstrates the way in which these traditional prejudices against women outside of the home transcend religion, transcend nationality, political systems, and the state of economic development. According to Professor Galenson, whether women work as doctors or scullery maids, not just in the United States, but throughout the industrialized world, she said: 'Women are at the bottom of the totem pole in the job market, regardless of the job.'

" . . . I don't care which country you would like to view—Britain, Sweden, Finland, Denmark—look at them. The problem is the same: the women at the bottom, the men at the top.

"So what are women going to do about it? What are we going to do about it? How are we going to change all that? How are we going to somehow reverse the trend that has women at the bottom of whatever profession we are talking about—a scientist or a physician or a scullery maid?

"It is going to take long, hard, slow, tedious work. And we begin with ourselves. We begin with our own self-concept. We begin to try to internalize how we really feel about ourselves and proceed to actualize the thinking that we finally evolve from the look inward and the projection outward.

". . . The women of this world—as the women of Texas, and the women of the United States of America—must exercise a leadership quality, a dedication, a concern, and a commitment which is not going to be shattered by inanities and ignorance and idiots, who would view our cause as one which is violative of the American dream of equal rights for everyone.

". . . We only want, we only ask, that when we stand up and talk about one nation under God, liberty, justice for everybody, we only want to be able to look at the flag, put our right hand over our hearts, repeat those words, and know that they are true."

But Congress was more than minority and women's rights legislation. It was more than twice monthly trips back to Houston to check things out with the home office, and feel the pulse of the constituents. Congress was also always politics. But Barbara had done her apprenticeship in the Texas Senate; she had no difficulty handling the same covert maneuvers on a national level.

As the *Wall Street Journal* (February 6, 1975) pointed out, she had become very knowledgeable at the game:

"Comet in Congress, Barbara Jordan's Star Reaches Dizzy Heights For a House Sophomore.

". . . Barbara Jordan certainly knows how to catch an audience's attention. That's she now, introducing Robert Byrd at the Democrats' midterm convention in Kansas City.

" 'Some will say that it is the depth of his intellect and capacity for human understanding and compassion. Others will say that it is his ability to lead other men and influence them to believe in the rightness of the cause he espouses. Some measure a man by the content of his commitment to a government of laws and others by his sense of justice . . .'

"Political rhetoric, yes, but Robert Byrd of West Virginia once belonged to the Ku Klux Klan, once called Martin Luther King a 'self-seeking rabble-rouser' and has voted against almost every major civil-rights bill. And Barbara Jordan of Texas is a black who is best known for her eloquent statement of constitutional principles during last summer's televised impeachment debate . . .

"So a lot of her fans are wondering why Rep. Jordan said all those nice things about Sen. Byrd.

" 'I really do believe that people change and that you can help people change more quickly at times, by defining them,' she replies. 'He was obviously moved by the introduction and said to me later: "You'll never be sorry that you introduced me." '

"Only time will tell whether Rep. Jordan's tongue is a magic wand in the case of Sen. Byrd. But the incident shows a side of Barbara Jordan not fully perceived by the public: She is a very ambitious politician who uses her eloquence not only on behalf of high principles but also to get ahead. Whatever his views on race, Sen. Byrd is, after all, No. 2 in the Senate Democratic leadership.

" 'If there's anything I can do for you,' he told her as they left the platform in Kansas City, 'don't hesitate to let me know.'

" 'And I won't,' Rep. Jordan added a month later.

"And she won't. For it isn't by hesitating that Rep. Jordan has achieved, in one congressional term, more honors and perhaps more power than most members of Congress can look forward to in a lifetime. . . ."

Her most controversial act while in Congress, and the one which drew the most fire, was the political decision to testify as a character witness for her old enemy, former Texas Governor John Connally. It was a small irony that Connally, having escaped the Sharpstown scandal at home, had landed in Washington in time to feel the breaking waves of Watergate and remained to be caught in a bribery charge in one retreating ripple known as the milk fund scandal.

David Broder, in *Atlantic Monthly* (March 1975), described the former governor's fall from grace:

"Connally was something special. Tall, handsome, polished, he moved easily in the worlds of politics and business. In Washington, Connally performed magnificently for Nixon, shaping and selling the 'New Economic Policy' that produced a bright flush of prosperity in 1972, then resigning from Treasury in time to head the 'Democrats for Nixon' organization in that year's campaign. The assumption that Nixon was grooming the Texan as his successor was well-established by the time Connally formally switched to the GOP in 1973.

"But Watergate was the death of such dreams. Connally's link to Nixon had undercut his presidential ambition even before he himself was indicted on charges of perjury, illegal payoffs, and conspiracy to obstruct justice in connection with an alleged Nixon campaign contribution from the milk producers . . . Connally's political hopes seem finished."

◾

People could not understand how, when he had ignored me so totally when I was in the Senate and he was governor for that one term, and when my eyes had filled with tears when he said what he did about Martin Luther King, that I would be a character witness for him in the bribery trial. Nobody could understand that.

At that time Nixon had resigned, Ford was the President, and Jaworski had wrapped up the business of his office. So we started to hear these murmurs and rumors and leaks that there was something coming out about John Connally, and that was all under the Special Prosecutor's office, which was still in existence.

Bob Strauss, who at that time was Chairman of the Democratic National Committee, asked me if I would testify as a character witness for Connally. Edward Bennett Williams, Connally's lawyer, had asked him to ask me.

My immediate answer was "No." But Strauss said: "Hold on, think about it. Think about it and see what you can say about it." So I agreed. Now that could not be a top-of-the-head decision, to be a character witness for John Connally. I thought about the matter for a week.

I went through the week thinking about whether I could testify as a character witness for John Connally. He had been Richard Nixon's Secretary of the Treasury. A Nixon appointee. At that point he was a Republican. I said in my head: "You can't refuse to testify for him because he is a Republican. That wouldn't make sense." So I dismissed the political factor, the change in party bit.

Still talking to myself, I asked: "All right, what is the question? What is the question you ask when you are a character witness?" I said: "Well, there's one question. What is this person's reputation for truth and honesty? Can you cite instances where John Connally has lied to you or been dishonest with you?" No, I couldn't think of anything. I thought of his saying when Martin Luther King died that those who live by the sword die by the sword. But that was his honest reaction. There was a crowd of people out there who heard him say that. That was the way he felt. It hurt me that he felt that way, but that was the way he felt.

I went through all those various things. I went back to the time in Texas. "Okay, you were in the state senate. What was your relationship with John Connally?" I answered: "He ignored me. Even when I held the key, he did." I reminded myself: "He ignored you, totally." So then it was clear that I owed him nothing. That made me a good character witness.

Then I asked: "Why would his lawyer want you to be a character witness for John Connally? That is obvious. You are being used by John Connally and his lawyer because this is an overwhelmingly black town, Washington, D.C., and you have this national reputation from the Nixon impeachment proceedings for fairness." All right, I knew in my own head that I was being used. That if I agreed to do this it would be an agreement to be used for that purpose. But I always made a distinction between when people used you and you didn't know it, and when you knew you were being used and agreed to it. I made that distinction then.

Finally, I asked myself: "Is there anything you want from John Connally? He's a Republican now, so he has lost his clout with the Democratic Party. There is not anything he can do for you politically."

In my time in Congress I had tried to build support across the board, so I would not have to rely on that band of liberals that I had relied on in 1962 when I lost. I had tried to expand this because I wanted conservatives and business types to become supportive of Barbara Jordan and not just to tolerate her. Of course it entered my mind that in testifying for John Connally that would certainly give me chits with them as somebody who was fair and open and not just locked into a knee-jerk position. And that would not hurt at all. I would be the person they could turn to when they were feeling guilty about anything they had done to others, and be redeemed. So that was certainly operative.

And then I got into the law and the ends of justice being served, and no matter how schmaltzy that may sound, I thought about that. That this man was on trial and a guilty verdict could be the end of him. Did I want to help see that the verdict was guilty? Or would I do anything to see that at least there was a fair chance that the jury weighed whatever the evidence was? I asked: "Now, you don't know whether he's guilty or innocent of the bribery, but would your participation in that trial do anything to insure fairness?"

All right, I had decided then that I ought to go ahead with it. There was really no good reason why I shouldn't do it. The hue and cry from the liberals in my district would certainly be there, but I could live that down. That would not bother me.

I decided to ask the question of all my friends; to seek their advice to see what they thought, not telling them that I had already settled the matter. So I talked to Nancy and various colleagues in the Congress, presenting this as a question that I didn't know what to do with. And getting feedback. I did a lot of that, even though I had already decided what I was going to do.

I told Bob Strauss that I would do it. And Bob said: "Thought you might."

Then one evening, in my apartment, John Connally called. Not his secretary, nobody between the two of us, just John Connally calling Barbara Jordan to say: "Thank you." Edward Bennett Williams had told him that I would testify as a character witness for him. "All right, Governor," I said. "I wouldn't have done it if I didn't feel it was the right thing to do."

I guess I got six letters from people in opposition. There was no big hue and cry after all.

■

But it stuck in the throat of a few. Two years later (May 9, 1977), *Encore* magazine still called Barbara's decision "a fissure in the solid wall" of black loyalty.

"It was her testimony on behalf of John Connally during his indictment in the milk fund scandal. Connally may have many admirable qualities, but one of them is not empathy with the black community. As governor, he fought to minimize voter registration and dismantle LBJ's Great Society Program. And many in Texas remember a statewide television broadcast in which he promised to use all the powers of his office to fight against a public accommodations bill guaranteeing blacks access to public facilities.

". . . Not surprisingly, Connally has nothing but praise for Jordan now. 'She is a woman of high principles, and yet she has learned that it's not enough to be an ideologue—that a degree of pragmatism must enter into one's life. She has intelligence, ability, and has always reflected excellent judgment.' (Which of these characteristics made her testify in front of a 12-member jury that included 10 blacks is still up for debate.)

"Jordan has won another political chip, but one can't help wondering at what personal price."

At the start of Barbara's second term in Congress, Texas

was resurrecting the frequently floating consideration of dividing itself into five states: ostensibly because of regional differences over water usage and utility regulation; in truth, because politicians could see the chance to become one of the five governors and ten senators from the new territories.

In Washington, native daughter Barbara Jordan also dwelt on expansion: hers. Entrenched in Congress and the public consciousness, she began to worry about her weight.

Now wearing a Lane Bryant large size 24½ in her boxy suits, she became offended that the press, which had once used such words as "presence" and "carriage" to describe her, now used "hulking" and "massive," words which meant that big was not beautiful. "I did not like people saying I was fat; big to me was different from being fat. It's a downer. It's not an attractive thing. I had become a fat lady—that's not the word they used but it was obvious that's what they meant, because they did not present whatever words they used in a positive framework."

It did not help that back home her mother was saying she looked just fine, that she was built just like her Grandmother Jordan and looked just like her.

Resolved to take off a hundred pounds, Barbara, aided by Nancy, set goals and made graphs. She weighed every day and plotted each loss on her chart. (And if there wasn't a loss, she didn't record it.) To sweeten the prize, Nancy promised that if Barbara lost sixty pounds by the time of the Democratic Convention she would buy her a fancy new set of wheels, of the kind she had in the old days—a bicycle.

So Barbara began to figure out how it was you emerged from all that protective bulk. Showing results sooner than

she expected, she noted with relief that "you don't neces-
sarily have to stop eating for all time. You just have to eat
differently. You stop running in for little midnight snacks,
and you stop going to those cocktail parties and eating hors
d'oeuvres and then coming home to eat a big dinner."

By the end of 1975, with the Voting Rights Act passed,
and Connally acquitted, and the scales marking a steady
loss, she got a chance to have her new, slimmer self
premiered on prime-time television.

Bob Strauss had called her in Houston earlier in the year
to say that he was getting the Democratic Convention
lined up and wanted her to have a big part in it. Would she
serve as chairman of the Rules Committee? "Not on your
life," she told him. "Think about it," he suggested, as he
had when he called about Connally. "Think about it and
call me." "I'm not going to think about it, Bob. It's not
anything I'm going to call you back on this time. I'm not
going to serve as chairman of the Rules Committee and I
know that. Can you imagine all those little factions? I'd be
bogged down for the duration."

Later, at the start of the presidential election year, she
got a call from him in Washington saying he wanted to
come see her. This time, in her office, he asked her to be
one of the keynote speakers. "Not *the* keynote speaker. He
did not feel comfortable having me in the limelight alone.
There had been pressure from some of his advisers to
even things up. So I was to be on there with John Glenn.
'The newness of an astronaut,' he explained, 'plus the
newness of a black woman, that would be an unbeatable
combination.' So I said: 'All right, I'll do that for you.'"

That was the last thing in Strauss's plan for a spectacular
kickoff to the convention that she did agree to. He had
plans for her and Glenn to walk from their respective dele-

gations down the aisles, amid cheers, to the podium. This was vetoed at once. "Look, Bob, I've got this bad knee. There's this cartilage which is damaged, maybe permanently. I don't need to be walking through the crowd on this knee." She also did not need to confide to him that surgery had been suggested, or that if she hadn't got so heavy to begin with it would never have got in that shape. It took enough pride to mention the matter to him at all, a matter that he should have perceived for himself, seeing her hobble on that leg.

So he altered his plans so that Glenn would come from the Ohio delegation and Barbara would appear on the podium from backstage.

Then there was the matter of the teleprompter. The day before the convention the technician asked her to come practice her speech with the twin machines, one set on each side to allow the speaker to move her head back and forth. "No way," she said. "I want my speech in front of me so I can turn the pages and see what comes next. I'm not going to look at a teleprompter."

But her speech was run through it anyway—because that was standard procedure.

The big night came: July 12, 1976. Barbara stood on the scales. Then, donning a new, smaller, light-green three-piece suit, she made her way to the convention. On the platform after Glenn's speech, during which the crowd had continued to talk among themselves and drown out the keynoter, Strauss tried to reassure Barbara that this inattention was the natural order of political gatherings—telling her not to worry, that the people in the hall were going to be walking around and talking and not paying attention; instructing her to concentrate on the seventy-five million viewers out there watching their TV sets.

But Barbara knew better. At the first sounds of her rising inflections, her sonorous repetitions, the hall grew silent as a church. "I looked up," she recalled, "and people were not milling around. All milling stopped. Now, really, the response was startling, as startling to me as that first standing ovation I got from the Harris County Democrats. Everything had been dullsville at the convention up to then, and I just thought: 'This is the way it will be.'"

Hunched over, reading through her new lightweight aviator glasses, she gave the throng one more First Time:

"One hundred and forty-four years ago, members of the Democratic Party met for the first time in convention to select their presidential candidate. Since that time, Democrats have continued to convene once every four years to draft a party platform and nominate a presidential candidate. Our meeting this week continues that tradition.

"But there is something different about tonight. There is something special about tonight. What is different? What is special? I, Barbara Jordan, am a keynote speaker.

"A lot of years passed since 1832, and during that time it would have been most unusual for any national political party to ask that a Barbara Jordan deliver a keynote address . . . but tonight here I am. And I feel, notwithstanding the past, that my presence here is one additional bit of evidence that the American Dream need not forever be deferred.

"Now that I have this grand distinction, what in the world am I supposed to say?

"I could easily spend this time praising the accomplishments of this party and attacking the Republicans, but I do not choose to do that.

"I could list the many problems which Americans have.

I could list the problems which cause people to feel cynical, angry, frustrated—problems which include lack of integrity in government, the feeling that the individual no longer counts, the reality of material and spiritual poverty, the feeling that the grand American experiment is failing or has failed. I could recite these problems, and then I could sit down and offer no solutions. But I do not choose to do that either.

"The citizens of America expect more. They deserve and want more than a recital of problems . . ."

Then, after a recitation of what the Democratic Party had stood for through the years—equality for all and privileges for none, that the gap between the promise and the reality of America could one day be finally closed—she ended, with all stops out, by quoting the man who freed the slaves:

"Now, I began this speech by commenting to you on the uniqueness of a Barbara Jordan making the keynote address. Well, I am going to close my speech by quoting a Republican President, and I ask that as you listen to these words of Abraham Lincoln you relate them to the concept of a national community in which every last one of us participates: 'As I would not be a *slave*, so I would not be a *master*. This expresses my idea of democracy. Whatever differs from this, to the extent of the difference, is no democracy.'"

The crowd went crazy, stomping and yelling and waving banners, chanting "WE WANT BARBARA" as she went to watch herself reviewed by Walter Cronkite, and to mosey up to the VIP lounge to the waiting arms and adulation of the Democratic National Committee. Glenn forgotten, Strauss was claiming credit for a convention gone wild. "I told these sons-of-bitches she'd be the hit of the show. I told them."

Jimmy Carter called to say that if he got the nomination he certainly hoped she would support him, and Barbara said that of course he knew he already had her support.

Everyone surrounded her, making over the new darling of the party. "They were all kissing my ass, that's all I can say about that time."

The next day's papers seized upon her as the delegates had done.

In the Philadelphia *Evening Bulletin* (July 13, 1976), columnist Sandy Grady reported:

"The Democrats were losing to boredom, 1–0, last night when they had the good sense to bring Barbara Jordan off the bench.

"Miss Jordan, as the ballplayers say, took it downtown. She tore it up. Grand slam.

"Jimmy Carter, watching the Democrats' lovefest on TV in his Americana Hotel suite, could only feel lucky he won't have to follow Barbara Jordan's act for three days. Getting on the same podium with Miss Jordan is like trying to sing-along with Marian Anderson."

The New York *Times* (July 13, 1976) recapped the story for its readers:

"It is a classic American success story: A poor child of extraordinary intellect, driven by parents who sought a better life for their offspring; an ambitious student who turned to the study of law because it seemed to provide the key to influence; a young politician who, not despairing after defeats in two attempts for public office, was elected on the third try; a state senator and then a member of Congress, who sought out and gradually won the confidence of the powerful and who was not beneath compromising and making deals to win some of that power.

"It was, in short, the road to success that white men had traveled since the country was founded."

Under a full front-page headline, the Washington *Star* raved:

"She was there to bear witness to a dream they yearn to claim, and the congregation responded with an 'amen' chorus that would do credit to the Second Coming.

"The Democratic Party, which has been at this convention business for 144 years, never had an opening night like this before, and never will again."

The Houston *Post* claimed their own:

"A poor kid from Houston's Fifth Ward sealed her destiny as a national superstar . . .

"They jumped and cheered and clapped and stomped and yelled—and loved her."

The Washington *Post* (July 14, 1976) in its lead editorial wrapped it up:

"The Texas delegation was on its feet cheering wildly, and so was just about everyone else in the hall—Florida and

South Carolina making a particular ruckus. The lone-star flag was being brandished with almost aggressive enthusiasm, and there on the platform stood two Texans taking the cheers: the son of a Jewish small businessman [Strauss] and the daughter of a black preacher. If the women's movement hadn't made it something of an offense to repeat, we know what we'd say to the Democrats: You've come a long way, baby."

By morning a full-fledged drive was under way to put her on the ticket as Vice President. Carter was inundated with telegrams, she with phone calls asking if she would accept the spot if it were offered.

By afternoon she had Bud get in touch with Jody Powell to say that if his people wanted to stop the groundswell and ease the candidate's mind, he could find them a room in which to have a press conference.

Addressing the matter in a prepared statement, she said: "It is improbable that Carter would take the bold, daring, unconventional, and un-southern move of naming a black or a woman as his running mate. Certainly not both at once." Alluding to a list of fourteen possible running mates, she commented that the list seemed more political than substantive, adding that she did not wish to be a token, that when her name got before a national convention she hoped it would be not to raise some issues but to elect her to some post. "It is not my turn," she said. "When it's my turn, you'll know it."

Nothing dampened the fans, however, and on the last night of the convention, as she and Martin Luther King's father ("Daddy" King), and vice-presidential candidate Mondale, and all the inner circle gathered around Carter on the platform, arms raised, to sing "Happy Days Are Here Again"—the hall was still filled with cries of "WE WANT BARBARA."

But she was no longer there. The event was over; it was time to return to Congress. Two unsettling sidelights had detracted from the main event.

One was the fact that Strauss had come up to her after the keynote address to say that he was glad that he and Edward Bennett Williams had not messed her up for all time by having her testify for Connally. "I felt doubly used by that situation to discover that he had seriously thought it might damage my career but had asked me anyway. I was angry that he had not leveled about what reservations he had."

The other letdown was the fact that she had lost her bet to Nancy: the scales on the big day had shown her three pounds too heavy. And no amount of explaining these away, or wheedling that it was close, got any results. Nancy would not budge; and Barbara was not going to get her new bicycle.

This vexation was softened somewhat the following week when she saw that her long siege of dieting had not gone unnoticed after all.

The Houston *Chronicle* (July 19, 1976) ran side-by-side photos of her, captioned *A Svelte Jordan*, with this story:

"Rep. Barbara Jordan of Houston has lost weight. She is shown at right in a photo taken September 12, 1975. At left is the trimmed-down Jordan pictured in New York as she attended the Democratic National Convention. Jordan

would not comment on the change. Aides said she simply
ate less than before."

Even more pleasing was the outrage of her faltering,
unknown opponent from the Eighteenth Congressional
District, who was opposing her in the general election for
her third race. To him this write-up, coming after a week
of steady convention coverage, was too much to bear in silence.

In the *Chronicle* column "Viewpoints," Sam Wright,
Republican, unloaded his ire:

"During my uphill fight to unseat Rep. Barbara Jordan,
I have had to sit by while my opponent has received national coverage as a possible vice-presidential candidate,
watched while she has been featured as a symbol for blacks
and women and read her opinions on topics varying from
Nixon's trip to China to Ford's chances for re-election. But
when you recently printed a story focusing on her tremen-
dous weight loss and illustrated it with before and after
photos, that was the last straw!

"How can a responsible candidate from a major political
party get a fair hearing when his opponent's every word
and action is splashed across the newspapers and his own
candidacy is ignored? To date, few people could probably
tell you whom Jordan is running against.

"It is true that I am running an underdog, poor-man
type of campaign while Jordan is receiving the support of
special interests, but a responsible newspaper is still obliged
to provide balanced reporting. While I realize that you
cannot ignore news, I think you can at least focus on some
of the issues of this campaign and get both sides of the
coin.

"Let's get down to the nitty-gritty and speak to these issues. I hardly think it's significant whether my opponent has lost weight or not—or at least it shouldn't be significant as regards her qualifications as a congressperson."

The reason the three pounds had not slipped away, or rather, had slipped back on, was that the week before there had been too much barbeque. The week before the convention had been the first annual around-the-clock, all-weekend-picnic-on-the-ground, for Barbara's oldest friends from Houston, at Nancy's house in Austin.

All of them, loyal for years, had come to every swearing-in, every official ceremony in Austin and Washington, and now they had been invited to be a part of her present private time.

They had also been invited to see the new house, going up on five acres next door, that Nancy and Barbara were building.

Three years before, Nancy Earl, who had a master's degree in educational psychology from Indiana University, had left her job at the University of Texas Measurement and Evaluation Center to move back to upstate New York and counsel students at Keuka College, where she had spent her undergraduate years.

But after a year and a half of cold winters she had come home again. Introspective, perceptive, Nancy realized that she needed to put her own roots down in the Onion Creek area that she loved. A young woman at forty-two, tanned and tow-haired, she wanted to pick watercress in the shade of cypress trees, plant grass on the back slopes, be outdoors when she was not in the professional situation of her job.

She was able to buy three and a half acres, and then another one and a half, adjoining the property her rent house was on. Barbara, loath to spend money for anything but what was solid and could be driven or walked upon, decided she wanted in on the house, too. It would be someplace for her that was not her mother's house on Campbell Street, someplace that would allow her a total retreat from her public life.

Plans had been drawn up in 1975, and when the ground was broken in 1976, the Bicentennial Year, a celebration was called for.

■

So we bought the property and were building the house and my mother and family could not get ready for my becoming a co-owner of a house. Mother said: "If you want a place, why don't you go out and find a place in Houston that's yours?" I tried to tell them the advantages of being out and away, of having someone who would be there all the time to see that the place didn't deteriorate while I was in the Congress. I explained that I would be a one-half owner, which means they would certainly be free to come. I invited them to come see for themselves.

So the whole group came on the Fourth of July. The Bicentennial. They had come for all my political events, but this was a party. That was the sole purpose of their coming, for a party. Two or three of them had been there for dinner, but this time it was everyone. So the campers and the overnight bags and all of it moved in because we were ready to celebrate the Bicentennial for as long as it took for us to get it properly celebrated.

We had bunting and flags all the way down the farm road, and then at the end of it one of my campaign placards to say that they were at the end of the trail. To let them know they had arrived.

And I had my sisters organize the group in Houston for

the trip and decide what we were going to have at various meals and who was going to bring what and that sort of thing. Now Bennie and Rose Mary do not have children, and so when they were not teaching they were running around taking care of the Deltas and Top Ladies of Distinction, because they liked to do that. And they were always the chief organizers for these affairs of mine.

They came, with their husbands, and Shirley and Wiley Word—later friends who enjoy us and we enjoy them—and the Justices and their husbands, and other special folk. We felt our group was very select, and we were protective of it. Most of us had known each other for the past forty years, and we all had fun together.

On the third of July we started our celebration with everybody moving outside to cook steaks. On the Fourth we barbequed steaks, chickens, ribs, and sausage. People brought cakes and pies, and we cranked homemade ice cream, which was always a treat.

We had a few fireworks that Nancy's boss and his kids brought, but it rained so it was too wet to shoot them off.

So the food was set out, and then we gathered around the rented piano in Nancy's sunroom, because the Justices liked to sing—Muriel, Evelyn, Mary Elizabeth, Norma, and Anna Lois—and the Jordan sisters—Bennie and Rose Mary and I—had to sing. That was always the way we topped off the evening. At first we all sang together. We sang spirituals and the "Battle Hymn of the Republic," things like that. Then we each did our specialty. My numbers, which I always did, were "Sunny" and "St. James Infirmary Blues." I didn't remember the words as I had had some drinks at that point, but that never deterred me. I could always make them up to fit. From year to year they changed, but it was always the same tune. Then I played my guitar. I never play well, but it was like my singing, ceremonial. Barbara will play her guitar whether you want to listen or not.

So we enjoyed each other all weekend, and exhausted ourselves having a good time. Eating and singing and dancing and a little drinking. And not much sleep.

Everybody retired and pretended to sleep for two or three hours, some of them up the road where they had motel rooms, but then we started in again with breakfast. I always cook the breakfast, bacon and eggs and biscuits, because everybody likes my eggs—scrambled eggs with cheese and chives. We borrowed a coffee pot for those who had to have coffee. And that meal lasted all morning.

So we had a good time, because they are all good folk.

4 July 1976
Dearest Nancy,

Thank you so kindly for the invitation to the nation's most fulfilling bicentennial celebration. It was a blast! We are convinced that out of all the celebrations happening simultaneously in the United States, ours was the greatest and the most unique.

Barbara is our most precious possession: our sister, our congresswoman, and our friend. We shall be eternally grateful to you for your providing such a picturesque setting for our celebration of the nation's birthday and of our friendship.

Until we meet again,

The Justice Sisters
and
their Husbands.

9. EXIT

After the keynote address, voters, disappointed that Barbara had not got the vice-presidential nomination and clamoring for her to take a post in the Carter cabinet, offered their free advice:

"Have suggested you for Director, Federal Bureau of Investigation. Please think about it."

"The United Nations is a dying horse. So why saddle yourself to an ineffective institution?"

"This white man from Alabama thinks you are the best choice for Ambassador to the United Nations."

"I am 17 years old and a great admirer of yours. I am writing you today because I heard on the news that President-elect Carter is considering you for Attorney General. I'm afraid I can't say things the way I want to, but I think it is very important for you to take the position."

"The press reports you have been offered the second spot of the Carter Presidential administration if he wins the election which is unlikely, for Gov. Carter has been deceiving the American peoples by omitting telling them he fronts for the 'insiders' who are plotting world control under the British Empire which is controlled by Pharisee Jews of the House of Rothchilds."

"I feel that you would be an asset in the office of Attorney General in the new administration. God in Heaven knows we need someone in the Country to help it go forward and not backwards. Someone who has insight to see more than just a dollar bill!"

Barbara's mind was elsewhere. To her the idea of a cabinet post seemed to offer nothing more substantive than another First Time. More immediate, and therefore more real to her, was the campaign trail with its familiar thrill of bringing audiences rising to their feet. But equally immediate, and more important, was the growing feeling that if she was to give her whole attention to what she did, she did not want to spend the rest of her life in the Congress of the United States.

Carter called me one day when he was getting his campaign all together and I was on the floor of the House and he said: "I want your help." And I said, and it's probably the third time I'd said that: "Well, as I told you, Governor, you've got my help. Just tell me what it is you want me to do." And he said that he would send his men to Washington to talk to me about it and we could outline a schedule. That sort of thing. I told him: "I will help as much as I can with your campaign, consistent with my own efforts, as I am running for re-election at the same time and I have an opponent." (Actually, my opponent was of no consequence. Nobody knew him. He had issued a release that he was going to run against Barbie Doll. It was all kind of a joke.) I made that decision to help Carter get elected because in those two terms in Congress I had had Richard Nixon and Gerald Ford, and I thought: One experience that you ought to have is to serve in the Congress with a Democratic President.

So Carter sent his men to Washington and they worked out, with Bud, a schedule sending me into Pennsylvania, New York, Ohio, Indiana, California—all the big states he needed. And I developed this standard campaign speech that I would always give, but then I would put in some ad-libbing. I would tell them that I'm endorsing Carter and I think you ought to vote for him because he's a good man and deserves your vote.

When all of it was over, I remember saying to Bud and Nancy that I don't know whether Carter ought to thank me for campaigning for him, or I ought to thank him for sending me to these places to campaign because I was having a ball. The reaction to me was what turned me on. I really enjoyed that. One time a student at Ohio State University got up and said something like: "You know, you're telling me to vote for Jimmy Carter and I guess I will, but I sure would feel a lot better if I was voting for Barbara Jordan for President." And that one just brought the house down. That really wiped them out. Those speeches didn't hurt me at all, and I think they helped Mr. Carter. I'm sure they did.

We would always end up with a question-and-answer session at those speeches; the audience would just go great guns. And at these, it was inevitable that someone would stand up and say: "Are you going to be Attorney General in Carter's cabinet?" "Are you going to be appointed Supreme Court Justice when Carter's President?" "Are you going to be Secretary of HEW?" Speculation would go on and on and the press would pick this up: "What will Barbara Jordan be in the Carter Cabinet?"

What no one seemed to understand was that it had not occurred to me that I would be anything in a Carter cabinet; I was primarily concerned with serving my third term in the Congress. But when I kept reading this, I thought: "Well, what would I do if I were asked?"

So then I started to give that some thought. And the question every day was: "What would you do?" So I thought about it, and I talked to my friends. What did they think? I had no trouble focusing on the things I *didn't* want to do. I knew lots of things I didn't want to do. I didn't want HEW; a black woman head of HEW couldn't do a thing that would be of interest. I was not interested in the U.N. at all, not at all. There was nothing I had ever done that would show an interest in foreign-policy initiative. So we finally decided, my friends and I: Look, you're a lawyer and if you do anything it ought to be in your field, and you ought to be head of it. What we came to then was that if the position of Attorney General was offered, I would consider that. But nothing else. And that's where we stood, although I knew that making that decision was like saying I was not going to be a member of the Carter cabinet.

Then Carter called me at my apartment in Washington, to say he would be in town and to ask if I would be interested in talking about a position in his administration, or if I would prefer to stay in the Congress. I said to myself: "Well, an either-or question like that is not exactly an offer of a position." But I told him: "Certainly, I'll talk to you about a position." He said: "All right, I'll call when I get to town."

Which he did. And I met with President-elect Carter at Blair House. There was nothing secret about that meeting. It started out with just the two of us initially. He said: "Now, you know I need some guidance, Barbara. I'd prefer it if you would give me several things that you would be interested in." And I told him my feeling. I said: "I would like to be able to give you several things but I don't have them, Mr. Carter. There is just one thing that I would consider. I wouldn't consider anything else but Attorney General." And then we chatted around about that, and he felt me out about some other things anyway. Did I have an interest in United Nations? I said: "I have no interest." He asked me about Solicitor General—he's the lawyer who brings the Government's cases, who's under the Attorney General—and I told him that I didn't have enough trial practice experience to be Solicitor General. Besides, it was under the Attorney General. He didn't broach the matter of HEW. Then he called in Hamilton Jordan and Vice President-elect Mondale, and he stated my position to them on Attorney General to let me know that he understood exactly what it was. And I considered that it was absolutely perfectly understood.

Then we chatted about other people that he was thinking about appointing to various other things, and the meeting was concluded. The story came out that our meeting ended earlier than it was scheduled for—well, that's because there wasn't much to talk about. Then a further story came out saying that we were not comfortable with each other, that we didn't get along, and the Black Caucus people got very upset because they thought some of the Carter people were trying to do me in with those stories. Carter called to say he had heard all this complaining and that he didn't have anything to do with those stories. And I said: "I didn't either, Mr. Carter."

Now, Black Caucus members were meeting with Carter in Plains, Georgia, about appointment of blacks to various things, but I didn't go to Plains; I announced early on that I was not going to Plains to talk about anything. I felt that if half a dozen members of the Black Caucus were going, there was no necessity for one more voice to say the same thing. And certainly Plains is not the easiest place in the world to get to. Besides, I had decided: If Carter wants me, he can call.

So that was how I was not in the Carter cabinet.

Now, in 1977, Carter had been elected President and I had been re-elected to the Congress, and at the start of that year I felt myself in a different kind of role in that third term.

By that time I could read that I was a national figure and not flinch, because I was a national figure, and people had heard about me all over the country. So what had to be considered was: What does one do now? Well, I had a real sense that ultimately a woman or a black would be the President or the Vice President, but not now. So I was not thinking in those terms.

Although I was still very junior in the Congress, I had begun to feel very senior. I felt that I had been in the

Congress many more years than I had been. What started to creep into my thinking was the question: How many times do you repeat these performances? How many times do you keep presenting a bill and getting it passed and getting the President to sign it? How many pens do you want?

I felt more of a responsibility to the country as a whole, as contrasted with the duty of representing the half-million people in the Eighteenth Congressional District. I felt some necessity to address national issues. I thought that my role now was to be one of the voices in the country defining where we were, where we were going, what the policies were that were being pursued, and where the holes in those policies were. I felt I was more in an instructive role than a legislative role.

I felt this when I met with my legislative assistant to talk about the program for 1977. And the issues that I started to address—other than applying the scheme for civil rights enforcement, that I had begun with LEAA, across the whole bureaucracy—were the economy, and high medical costs that the whole country was suffering from, and the matter of how we could bring down these escalating prices with the President's cost-contained program. I wanted to do something about that.

At that time I was declining 99 per cent of the speeches that I was requested to make, and was accepting only those that were national in scope, that provided me with an opportunity to make some kind of a policy statement about the country. I gave a speech to the American Pharmaceutical Association; and one to Tufts University doctors, on nutrition and preventive medicine. So I could see myself moving in a different direction, into a different role.

There had always been many requests for commencement speeches. And I had done a lot of those; had been awarded, at that juncture, twenty-two doctoral degrees, including one at Boston and one scheduled at Princeton. So I was thinking: "Well, maybe I don't need to do any more of those. How many commencement speeches do you give? How many honorary degrees do you want?"

Then I got a letter from Harvard University. It had voted to give me an honorary doctoral degree at its June commencement. So I answered myself: "Well, that's one you take. How many more? One more." That was simple. One more. I put the notation on the letter: "Tell them, Yes, I'll be there. I will accept. Advise me of the details later."

My office staff was kind of slow and I would check periodically—"Has the letter gone out to Harvard?"—because I didn't want those people to change their minds. But it had gone out, so that was fine, and I was going to Harvard to receive an honorary degree.

About a month passed, and there was a second letter from Harvard, saying that they would like me to give the commencement address at that same occasion. Well, I was very pleased by this. And reading their letter of invitation, which said how George Marshall used that opportunity to announce the Marshall Plan, I had the Library of Congress send over the Marshall Plan.

I knew I was going to have to give my full attention to writing that speech. I thought about that: Was there time to devote to getting that all together? But I knew that if I declined I was going to be very disappointed with myself; I knew I would not be comfortable with that decision. So I thought: I'll do it. I told Bud: "Tell them, Yes. Letter will follow."

I would think about the speech periodically and what I

could say that hadn't been said so many times before. Well, everything has been said lots of times.

But there was one thing that annoyed me in terms of what we were doing in the Congress: We were always mouthing about citizen participation, citizen involvement. We talked about it, but then I could see that my colleagues did not really want citizens to participate. They really didn't trust the people to have anything worthwhile to offer; they thought the people were more of a nuisance than a help. I decided: "Well, I can talk about that." So you're halfway there once you decide that you know what you're going to talk about. The rest is just putting it together.

While I worked on this matter it occurred to me that, with the kind of publicity I had received and the kind of platform I could mount, such as I was doing then, that I didn't need to be an elected public official in order to say those things, or address those problems in any national or global way.

That, as a matter of fact, being an elected public official took time away from the time I would otherwise have to think about other problems and address specific problems, because it was easy to become bogged down in the minutiae of committee meetings and settings and roll-call votes and quorum calls, and spend many hours doing things that you really had no interest in doing.

I was writing this speech to say that the people were supposed to govern, and I didn't feel that I could really generate that kind of citizen participation from within the constricting office of an elected official.

I was now convinced that I had reached a point where my words were going to be heard and attended to, whether I prefaced my name with Representative,

Congresswoman, Senator, or whatever. And if I had reached that point, then I didn't have to be a part of those political institutions which demand so much of your time in a routine way. I believed that in order to free myself to move fully in a new direction, I would of necessity have to leave elected politics and pursue the platform wherever I could find it. And I was thinking at that point, working on the Harvard speech, that the platform would be presented to me, that it wouldn't be difficult to find.

So the thing to do, I told myself, was not to run for re-election for a fourth term, but rather to free my time in such a way that it could be structured by the country's needs as I perceived them. I decided to move in a new direction.

The question was: "How do I effect this?

▪

Except for a Polsky Morgan painting of a tender black man bending over a small black girl, Barbara's private office seemed empty of her. It was a formal place for public matters—a long way from the place on Onion Creek with its cypress and watercress. Visitors sat in navy leather armchairs; she sat behind her massive walnut desk, usually in a workday ultrasuede jumper and blouse.

In the outer office a staff—consisting of personal secretary, a caseworker who dealt with the problems of voters back home, and a receptionist—confirmed appointments, dealt with visitors from the Lone Star state, and handled the steady flow of tourists and journalists who wanted to sit beneath the stern Avedon portrait of the congresswoman and pore over her scrapbooks. In the back office, legislative assistants worked on speeches and bills. The no-risk mood of post-Watergate Washington had affected them all. Her assistant, Bud Myers, liked to hark back to the more idealistic years of the Great Society when "every vote was greeted with cheers or tears," or even to what he called the "street years," which at least had had the vigor of protests and marches. Yet, chided by a constituent for the impersonal tone of office letters—for a reply to a man who had written that his brother had lost both legs and had "always been rooting for you, Barbara," that began, "Yours of the 25th received"—Bud shrugged the matter away. "You don't want to set up a personal relation with the writer; you don't want him to think you've established rapport."

Most of the time in the private office, Barbara was on the telephone, dealing, as she did on the floor of Congress, with the daily inching along of minority rights and women's matters. These calls took place against a background jangle of bells—that elaborate scheme of long and short rings which advised all congressional members of calls to session, quorum notices, and record votes.

With a caller, she reviewed a letter signed by her and fifteen other Black Congressional Caucus leaders, addressed to the President, protesting the Government's *amicus curiae* brief in support of Allen Bakke in his case against the University of California at Davis:

"We understand that the brief takes the position that the University of California acted in an unconstitutional and discriminatory manner in its establishment of a special-admissions program to benefit economically and socially disadvantaged applicants to medical school. We strongly oppose this position apparently taken by the government. This position is not only contrary to the relevant civil rights law, but will also have the effect of irretrievably undermining the affirmative action program to benefit public and private entities.

"We urge the administration to reconsider and reverse its reported decision to support Allan Bakke's position in this case. As indicated in the memorandum left with you at our meeting Wednesday, we believe that future generations would come to regard a government brief supporting Bakke's position in the way the nation would now view a government brief in support of segregation in *Brown* v. *The Board of Education*. A government brief opposing affirmative action programs would be a statement to the black community indicating the government's reversal of its commitment to civil rights in this country."

Over the phone she argued that there were lots of ways to test applicants: "There's empathy quotient . . ."

Barbara's only real privacy in Washington was in her muted black-and-tan, high-rise apartment, which had a view of the Capitol but was far enough from it for escape. There, beneath a painting of an old black couple in a horse-drawn wagon, she could be alone and catch her breath. Or, on the rare occasions when close friends visited, talked over barbeque and scotch about whatever came to mind, whatever was personal and apart from legislation.

Her weight, in 1977, was still high priority. She complained: "Mother says, 'You're looking like a scarecrow.' She can't get a handle on it. I think that's a black thing, looking big and healthy. She simply can't understand it. I try to tell her other people are glad. Last week we went shopping in Houston after I made a speech, and I wanted to buy some panties, and the saleslady said: 'Oh, you look beautiful. How did you do that?' And I told Mother: 'You see what people say?' But she said: 'They don't know. People will think you're sick.'"

Money, its presence or absence, was frequently on her mind. "Right now I am very uncomfortable if I don't have any money. The whole feeling that a person ought to be able to pay his way is important to me. It gives me a feeling of power in myself. My great longing during the entire time I was in school was that one fine day I was going to get to the place where I could earn money enough to make me feel comfortable all the time. When I first started to earn money I used to carry around large sums of cash. I would carry hundred-dollar bills in my billfold every day just to have it there. Did I spend it? No. I would just open my billfold from time to time and look at it. I was doing that when I realized that it was unsafe. So I don't do that; but I still keep more money than I should in checking accounts. I know the money in the checking account is not earning a cent, but a part of having money is to keep a large checking account—because then those pieces of paper in my checkbook represent access to cash, and I like ready access to cash.

"Money really was important to my Grandfather Patten and it was important to my father, he enjoyed making money, and it now is to my mother. Of course she never had any money of any consequence throughout her life; she grew up very poor. But after my father's death, all his money became hers, and she doesn't like to part with any of it. When she acquired my Cutlass—she doesn't drive but she likes to have a car sitting there—she said: 'This is a small car. Your father always drove big cars.'

"It is very difficult for me to part with large sums of money. Of course I don't mind spending money for cars or clothes, but I know that if I'm going to part with a large sum I'll have to think about it for a week or so, and I will delay until the last moment writing the check, even though it's something that I would like to do, and know in my head that I am going to do. For instance: The purchase of my one-half interest in the land in Austin. I guess I thought about that, and turned it over in my mind, for a month before I ever did it. It was a large expenditure. But ultimately I enjoyed spending the money on that, because then I could walk around those acres and say: 'This is mine.' I had to get it firmly fixed in my mind just what the dimensions of that property were. I enjoy the house; I enjoy walking around the land. I enjoy spending the money on furnishings once I get over agonizing that I have to write a check. The things I enjoy spending money on are definitely those things which bring me personal ownership pleasure.

"My family says that I am very stingy. That's the way they describe me when it comes to money. That I am very reluctant to part with one dollar for some cause that they think I should part with it for. For instance, Rose Mary said some weeks ago that I ought to be a life member in the Delta sorority, and that was a five-hundred-dollar membership. I told her it would be safer for our relationship if she never mentioned that to me again in my lifetime."

The conversation, when it strayed to politics, was always about what lessons she had learned, never about the content of her congressional work. "I have discovered how to be discretionary in terms of who is permitted to use me and who is not. I learned that concerning Connally. Those trade-offs are part of politics. Now, last week I got a call from the White House. The President, someone relayed, wanted me to go to New Jersey to help the candidate for governor. The President had already been there. They wanted me to go. Now, I didn't know the man who was running, so that was not important. It was the White House calling—that was what was important. I asked myself: 'What do I get in return?' My exchange of favors was not with the candidate for governor of New Jersey, but with the White House. Well, I had already done my thing for Carter at the time of the campaigning and helping with the election. And I hadn't called in any of those chits at that point. I decided: I don't need to stockpile favors at the White House, so I won't go to New Jersey. That's just politics."

Barbara enjoyed it when friends brought her new trivia concerning her public life that they had happened upon. It made her feel that she was with people she could trust to keep her at a distance from those she could not. Someone showed her the cover of *Encore* magazine (March 9, 1977), on which a set of pearls had been added to the picture.

"I don't own any pearls," she said.

"Maybe they thought you should."

One friend said, "I have a First Time for you, Barbara. The thirteenth edition of the National Green Book of Funeral Directors, Embalmers, and Florists is dedicated to you."

"Mother was right," she answered. "They think I'm not long for this world."

Traveling with her in public places was much like being part of the entourage of a film star in the forties.

After a speech to the Civil Rights Division of the Justice Department, headed back to the capitol, she was waylaid in the hallway. With aides on each side, she fended off strangers and acquaintances who tugged at her jumper, clawed her arms, and almost knocked her off balance as they touched, shouted, wheedled, pleaded for attention and favors.

As the elevator door closed her off from them, one aide said, "You've got to get out of this town."

"What did I tell you?" she answered.

The same pawing prevailed at huge galas as at those daily speaking and committee events. At the thronging Congressional Black Caucus, black tie, headliner dinner, she was the center of media attention as the glare of television lights picked up her long fluted peach dress; this interest, even though the hotel was filled with black luminaries—Alex Haley, Andy Young, Shirley Chisholm, Yvonne Burke—and a large sprinkling of white notables and officeholders wanting to be in evidence.

At her table, with Bud on one side, and an old Houston friend, Congregational minister Prentis Moore, on the other, she continued to be kissed, hugged, poked, pulled, and tugged by the people in the crowd calling, "Here's our Barbara," "Hey, you remember me, don't you?" "You promised to come by and you never did; now don't forget." All wanting to make contact.

At one point Barbara, to distract attention from herself, waved across the room. "There's Lou Gossett," she said, indicating the television star who had played Fiddler in *Roots*. ("*Fiddler on the Roof?*" murmured a disoriented white guest.)

The ultimate invasion of privacy, of adulation carried to the obscene, came after dinner, before the lengthy program. Deciding to locate a bathroom before the banquet hall doors were cordoned off for the arrival of President Carter—the principal and somewhat unpopular speaker—

Barbara slipped out into a long, carpeted hall, and walked its pillared distance to a mammoth space identified as LADIES.

There, women out in the mirrored lounge, touching up their make-up and smoothing carefully coiffed hair, heard a shriek from within: "Barbara Jordan used *my stall!*"

Harvard was different. There her public and private life merged. There, also, the past and future converged on her present.

Before the ceremonies, Barbara and Nancy and Bud rendezvoused with old Boston University friend Bill Gibson, early in a springlike June day.

"I thought him very handsome then," Barbara whispered as Bill helped her into his car to take her across the Charles River to their schooldays twenty years before.

"Don't let Barbara tell you that this trouble with her leg is new," he instructed her friends. "She didn't like to walk back then. She wouldn't go out to eat with us unless we could afford a cab."

In Boston he pointed out an old brick apartment building on a shaded street. "We used to throw parties at my place. They'd tap on the window and I'd let them in. We'd have Salisbury steak if things were tight, or go out for pizza when we could. We had a lot of fun."

Barbara could not respond to that. Rounding a corner, she looked up. "That's Beacon Hill. Where the law school was. That was a hard climb."

In the afternoon before the commencement excercises, she and her friends wandered through the tree-lined Harvard campus, mingling with the crowd of gowned graduates, alumni in top hats, the Radcliffe class of 1905 in flowered dresses, scholars in tinted hoods, students and professors wearing white armbands carrying banners which read END APARTHEID, and proud and sweating parents ready to take their seats and sing "Gaudeamus Igitur."

Nancy, Bud, Bill, and other old friends sat in roped-off chairs near the front, reading the program to get the feel of that prestigious school. A folder called *These Festival Rites* explained the order of the day:

"The Commencement Procession is formed in four Divisions: the candidates for Advanced Degrees assemble in the Sever Quadrangle. In the Old Yard are formed the Seniors, candidates for the A.B., the Alumni, and the President's Division. This last comprises three sections. The first is led by the Sheriffs of Middlesex and Suffolk Counties. The University Marshal then escorts the President and any Presidents emeriti who attend, followed by the other six members of the Corporation and by the Board of Overseers . . .

"The President's Procession is seated on the platform in front of the side porch of Memorial Church. The President sits in the center in a Jacobean chair which has been used at every Harvard Commencement since at least the time of President Holyoke in the eighteenth century, if not earlier."

The program began. "We hope to make our plenty fairly serve the needs of all," intoned someone in introductory remarks.

After the Latin Salutatory Disquisition, "Somnium Chaonis," a young Sicilian, Robert Mulé, stepped forward to give the English Valedictory Disquisition, "The Need and a Desire," ending it with a moving tribute to his father and the skill of his father's workingman's hands.

Behind these scholars, Barbara, ninety pounds lighter, in a black skirt and tucked white blouse beneath her academic robe, sat waiting on the platform. She looked like a student about to receive a prize. Beside her were the other honorees; singer Marian Anderson, novelist Eudora Welty, financier Albert Gordon, botanist Paul Mangelsdorf, lawyer-historian Paul Freund, Oxford scholar Sir Richard Southern.

The slow afternoon began to heat up and the rhetoric started to drag. Barbara leaned over to Harvard President Derek Bok and whispered: "I have a plane to catch."

Preceding her to the podium, he articulated the elitism that she had come to speak against:

" . . . There are certain advantages that are most likely to be found in the setting of a private university.

"To begin with, we have complete freedom to pick and choose the students we admit to Harvard College . . .

"There are great advantages in being free of the political control to which each public university is subject. Such freedom means independence from the shifting priorities of a state legislature . . . It gives us the freedom to set our own priorities and goals without competing for attention with the junior colleges and other institutions that make up a vast state system of higher education . . .

"In every generation, there are only a few scientists and scholars with the power and creativity to leave a lasting imprint on their fields of knowledge. For more than a century, the special quality of Harvard has been founded on our ability to attract a disproportionate share of these uniquely talented people . . .

"The mission of our great private universities has always been to establish standards that can inspirit higher education as a whole."

When Barbara's turn came, there was an acknowledgement of First Times: for a black woman to give the Harvard commencement address, for any individual to have been chosen both by the honorary degree committee and the speaker's committee.

Then, standing alone, her eyes looking past the alumni into the faces of the students, Barbara gave the speech she had spent so many hours preparing. In a fine historical juxtaposition, one member of the graduating class before her was Lisa Brown, youngest daughter of the woman who agitated and brought to bear the suit which became *Brown* v. *The Board of Education*.

"Mr. President, were I to begin what I am going to say this afternoon by starting out, 'I am very pleased to have been invited to speak to the Harvard community,' you would probably discount that as a trite beginning. But if you did that, you would be in error. I have always held Harvard in high regard. I have always viewed a Harvard education as an unexcelled badge of intellectual achievement—if not superiority. I've always felt that way.

"My appearance here this afternoon may not honor you very much, but it certainly honors me.

"You know, the truth of the matter is, that one of the reasons I attended Boston University Law School was because I wanted to be close to Harvard. But my earliest brush with Harvard occurred over twenty years ago. I was a junior at Texas Southern University. Now, I might add that the original name of TSU was Texas State University for Negroes. It was created to keep blacks out of the University of Texas. So a Harvard debate team came to TSU—a Harvard debate team. And I was a debater. And I couldn't understand why this institution so revered by me would send debaters to TSU. But they came anyway. And the debate occurred. And the judges said that the debate ended in a tie.

"Well, now, it occurs to me today that if Harvard students were so superior—or as superior as we all thought—they should have won. And since the judges said the debate ended in a tie, we must have won. So, Mr. President and all of the alumni, I hereby declare that when that debate was held over twenty years ago, we won. And if you have any surplus trophies around anywhere I'll take one home to the team. And if you should run into two gentlemen—one's name was Jared Diamond and the other, James Sykes—they were the Harvard debaters at that time, I invite you to offer them my condolences.

"I received a letter of invitation to make this speech today. And as I read it, it appeared designed either to challenge or intimidate. One or the other. I want to quote to you one unedited paragraph from the letter of invitation I received. Now listen to this:

"'We invite you to speak on whatever topic you find suitable. A number of Harvard Commencement speeches have been memorable.' That's not the end of the quote. It went on. 'Perhaps the most memorable was that of Secretary of State George C. Marshall, who used the occasion to announce the Marshall Plan for Europe.'

"Well, I read that, and, I can promise you, you're not getting a Jordan Plan today. I don't have a plan to create, ameliorate, eliminate, or anything else at this time, and if I happen to develop one at some time during the remainder of my life, I'll ask you to invite me back.

"Now, even though I will not present a plan to you this afternoon which will be celebrated thirty years hence, I will talk about a problem which concerns me greatly. The answers to this problem are not in the back of the book, and they're not at the end of this speech.

"Of late many articles have been written, and speeches delivered, about the importance of the input of people into the affairs of government—symbolic gestures have been staged, and populist rhetoric has been translated into law—the point of it all is to make people feel that they really do count. That the government does care what they think. Such actions are said to be the logical extension and proper fulfillment of an amorphous something called The Promise of America.

"Question: Do the governors of America sincerely believe that people are a valuable resource of the government? Or do the governors really believe that the people are merely an indispensable nuisance to a democracy?

"Let us reflect on our history for a moment and maybe we'll try to answer that question.

"The Declaration of Independence, the first sentence: 'When it becomes necessary for one people to dissolve the political bonds whenever government becomes destructive of certain unalienable rights, it is the right of the people to alter or abolish it.'

"And then, when they started to itemize the oppressiveness of George the Third: 'He has refused to pass other laws for the accommodation of large districts of people unless those people would relinquish the right of representation in the legislature—'

"It continues his invasions on the rights of the people: 'He has sent hither swarms of officers to harass our people. He has destroyed the lives of our people.'

"And then, finally, in the Declaration: 'It is made in the name and by the authority of the good people.'

"People.

"People, throughout it.

"Subsequently, the Constitution was written. It augmented and implemented the political philosophy espoused in the Declaration of Independence, the *raison d'être* of the new government.

"People again.

"'The political well-being of the people, the government's source of authority.'

"The people. Once more and again. The quintessence: 'We the People of the United States.'

"'The House of Representatives chosen every second year by the people . . . the right of the people peaceably to assemble . . . the people to be secure in their persons . . . the enumeration of certain rights retained by the people, and certain powers reserved to the people.'

"And then as the states began to ratify that Constitution a debate developed wherein a delegate wanted to strip Congress of the power to lay and collect taxes, and Alexander Hamilton, trying to allay the delegate's fear, addressed him, the proponent of the resolution. And what did Hamilton say? 'Here, sir, the people govern.'

"'Here, sir, the people govern!'

"Do you believe that?

"Do the people govern? Or has there been a mutation from a commitment to people to a commitment to self-interest on the part of the governors?

"Is the applause meter paramount, and the welfare of the

people, at best, merely tangential? The government has built an elaborate network of illusions. That network is designed to make people believe that their opinions are genuinely wanted and considered, that they do participate, in fact, in making the decisions of government.

"We go to great lengths to sustain that illusion.

"Prevalent phrases among some of the recent legislation the Congress has passed, phrases which are substitutes for people: Citizen participation, advisory council, advisory committee, maximum feasible participation, public participation, community participation, petition for intervention. The words are all there. But is citizen intervention encouraged or discouraged?

"Petitions to intervene: The citizen wants to intervene in proceedings of the Atomic Energy Commission and he goes to the rule book and asks: 'How do I intervene before this Atomic Energy Commission?'

"The rule is stated this way, it's headed 'Intervention':

" 'Any person whose interests may be affected by a proceeding and who desires to participate as a party shall file a written petition for leave to intervene. Any petition shall identify the specific aspect or aspects on which the subject matter of the proceeding as to which he wishes to intervene. He must set forth with particularity both the facts pertaining to his interest and the basis of his contentions with regard to each aspect on which he desires to intervene.'

"Now that clear paragraph is followed by seventeen sections and subsections. There are other regulatory agencies with rules equally as burdensome.

"The people have a right to intervene. Though statutory and regulatory language may well include provisions for petitions to intervene, the fact is that proper citizen intervention often requires an attorney or an expert witness.

"The citizen is denied the right to intervene.

"Getting into federal court, there is a $10,000 requirement that that amount must be in controversy before you can get in. The Supreme Court has said you still won't get in unless each member of the class satisfies that jurisdictional amount. The Court has ruled again that a person bringing a class action suit must notify all parties at his own expense.

"The Supreme Court has said only the Congress may authorize the payments of such fees, and Congress is very reluctant to do that.

"Have the Supreme Court decisions furthered opportunities for citizen participation? Well, recently the Supreme Court has acted to limit both the right to sue, and class action litigation. The Court has ruled, for one instance, that citizens and taxpayers have no standing to challenge an action of the government unless they can show a concrete injury in fact.

"Another ruling: That ghetto residents of Rochester lacked standing to sue because they could not prove that the alleged wrong hurt them personally. Another ruling: Plaintiffs must demonstrate that the complaint they offer is not simply arguable but actual.

"People.

"The people want in.

"How much longer, how much longer will people tolerate a network of illusions and vacuous rhetoric? How much longer?

"What the people want is very simple: They want an America as good as its promise. That's what they want.

"The people do not want to be outskirters. They want to be insiders on America.

"We want to be in control of our lives. Whether we are jungle fighters, craftsmen, company men, gamesmen, we want to be in control. And when the government erodes that control, we are not comfortable. We're not comfortable at all.

"I submit to you that the re-inclusion of the people in their government would be recombinant of predictable and laudable results. It would be a return of a right which we once considered unalienable.

"The stakes, the stakes are too high for government to be a spectator sport."

She spoke for seventeen minutes. Then, in contrapuntal confirmation of tradition, voices rose to sing the Harvard song:

Fair Harvard! thy sons to thy jubilee throng,
    And with blessings surrender thee o'er,
By these festival rites, from the age that is past
    To the age that is waiting before . . .

Be the herald of light, and the bearer of love
    Till the stock of the Puritans die.

The minister gave the benediction, and the afternoon was adjourned by the Sheriff of Middlesex County.

Hesitantly, the crowd came forward to her. It was as if no one else but Barbara Jordan had spoken. Young and old, black and white, academically gowned and top-hatted, barefooted, gray-suited, they all stood in orderly rings around her until there were hundreds pressing forward, all wanting the same things: to touch her, to speak to her, to get her scrawled "BJ" on their program.

As she and her friends walked back across the yard to her room in Harvard's guest house, one of the policemen escorting her said: "We haven't had a mob like that since the President was here."

It wasn't clear what President he meant; and maybe he didn't know himself. The President. Not since the Office of President had last been there had that scene been conjured forth.

Back in the room, in schoolgirl black and white, Barbara sank down in a chair. "I want a cigarette."

A friend produced one and she lit it.

Vexed that she had had to limp away from the ceremony, she removed her black calf pumps. "It was the shoes. If you hadn't made me wear these black ones to match my robe, Nancy—it was the toes. They ruined my toes."

Nancy dug out old comfortable brown shoes, a duplicate style, but well-worn. "You couldn't wear these on the platform."

"I don't know why not. They were not interested in my feet. They definitely were not."

What they had been interested in were her words. Earlier she had said that the trouble with President Carter was that he couldn't speak, that he didn't know how to project the passion and compassion which let you bring your audience into where you were. But she had done that; she had taken them back to the southern Negro college of her early days and led them to where they sat that day. She had led them from her past to their present.

"I had them, didn't I?" Barbara, too, thought of the crowd.

"You did."

"Sometimes I just stare in the mirror and look at myself and I say: 'Barbara, by golly you've done okay. It wasn't easy but you've done okay.' Tom Freeman told me I'd never get into Harvard, not to apply. But here I am. I did get in. Right now here I am. I'm in." She leaned back, bestowing her grace on those who had bestowed it upon her. "I like those folk. They're just like the Missionary Baptist Church, only they wear top hats."

"You got to meet Marian Anderson," Nancy reminded her.

"I did. And it was fine to be finally introduced to her. She told me it was a pleasure, but I told her that the pleasure was mine. I told her what it was like for us to hear her thirty years ago in those balconies."

"Her husband said they were going to invite you to visit."

"Yes, that she had always regretted that she had not asked Eleanor Roosevelt."

"It looked good to see you both sitting up there," someone said.

"Well, Harvard is a pinnacle. And the inclusion of Barbara Jordan and Marian Anderson guaranteed that."

They savored what her statements meant that afternoon in June.

"Where do you go from here?"

"That's always the question: What next?" Barbara considered. "One thing I know for sure: I'm going to buy myself a jeep."

"You could open a barbeque stand."

"Or start a Barbara Jordan money-belt franchise."

The light touch of her friends made Barbara feel secure. Their ease freed her to be serious.

"I don't know here this afternoon what will be next for me," she said. "I won't know what the next step is until I get there. I know that when I went to Boston, and Austin, and Washington, I took with me everything I had learned before. And that's what I will do this time. That's the point of it, isn't it? To bring all you have with you wherever you go."

Our thanks to
Attorney Bea Ann Smith.

The world's thanks to
Justice John Marshall Harlan.